Irish Thursdays

More Little Parables from Ireland

120 inspirational messages

Sally I. Kennedy

Irish Thursdays
More Little Parables from Ireland

By
Sally I. Kennedy

Copyright ©2007, Sally I. Kennedy
ISBN: 978-0-6151-4886-1

Also by Sally I. Kennedy:
52 Little Parables from Ireland
Kwackie the Wonder Duck
Words from the Heart
Poppy the Penguin®
Poppy and Pals

www.sallyikennedy.com
Tel. 561-912-9906
Fax: 561-912-9306
Email: SallyIKennedy@bellsouth.net

Cover and internal photos, © *Sally I.
Kennedy*

Daily Wisdom devotions from
2004-2006

Publishing services by

❖ *LotusBooks.net*

To Adrienne, David, Lisa, Todd,
Teri, and Benjie

Contents – Irish Thursdays

Section I

Give thanks to the Lord of lords.
His faithful love endures forever.   Psalm 136:3

A Second Touch

"Then... he saw everything clearly." Mark 8:25

In my younger days, it didn't matter if I got all the "face paint" on before heading out. Makeup just wasn't a priority. I felt okay with or without it. Nowadays, however, well that's another story.

This morning I was hurrying to finish getting ready. We were leaving for the weekend, and there would be no time later in the day to reapply the makeup. I kept messing it up while rushing.

"If the light was just a little brighter", I mused. I turned the rheostat up as high as it would go. There. That did help a little.

As I put the finishing touches on my makeup, I thought of the verse in the chapter of Luke that talks about seeing, but not clearly. I love that story. It's the one about a second touch from the Lord.

Believers in Jesus Christ as Lord and Savior are "in the light". Sometimes, though, we need a second touch from the Holy Spirit to help us see more clearly. Or sometimes even a third, or fourth, or hundredth.

The good news is the Lord is willing to do that at any time. We just have to ask.

A Little Bit of Shade

"How precious is Your lovingkindness, O God! And the children of men take refuge in the shadow of Your wings." Psalm 36: 7

Sometimes our summers (and falls!) are cookers. I have always been impressed by the difference just a little bit of shade makes. In the heat of the day, simply moving under a tree instantly creates a more comfortable feeling. There's less glare; it feels cooler.

There are many references in the Bible about being, hiding, and taking refuge, under the "shadow" of His wings. I have pondered that, from time to time, and never gotten a totally satisfactory answer.

One thing's for sure, a shadow, of a tree for example, provides shade. During times of intense heat (trouble), the shadow (shade) carries relief. It is a respite.

I love all the Psalms, and chapter 121 is no exception. In verse 5 it says, "The LORD watches over you, the LORD is your shade at your right hand."

What better place to catch our breath than in the shadow of God, or in the shadow of His wings? We can cool off, regather our wits, and get back out there.

Sometimes it's good to remember that a bit of shade is just the ticket, especially when the shade is from the shadow of our Heavenly Father. Psalm 121 1 says, *"I lift up my eyes to the hills where does my help come from? 2 My help comes from the LORD, the Maker of heaven and earth. 3 He will not let your foot slip he who watches over you will not slumber; 4 indeed, he who watches over Israel will neither slumber nor sleep. 5 The*

LORD watches over you the LORD is your shade at your right hand; 6 the sun will not harm you by day, nor the moon by night. 7 The LORD will keep you from all harm. He will watch over your life; 8 the LORD will watch over your coming and going both now and forevermore."

Antiques

"And when Jesus went into Peter's house, He saw his mother-in-law lying ill with a fever. He touched her hand and the fever left her; and she got up and began waiting on Him." Matthew 8

Thick dust covered the hand-hewn ridges in the simple cherry cupboard. This cabinet that my dad's grandfather had lovingly made, as a gift for his bride, was something priceless.

It was a simple piece of furniture, with two doors on the bottom, and two shelves on top, encased by very old glass doors. Originally it was made as a totally functional piece, to hold their dishes and kitchen ware, when they were first married.

The front was decorative, but the back was a flimsy plywood. The hardware needed replacing, too. When we moved it from my parent's home to our home, a big chunk of molding was missing from the front.

I was reluctant to give the job of restoration to just anyone. Finally we found someone in whom we had confidence, to restore and refinish this antique.

The refinisher was amazed at the incredible work on the original cabinet, and how marveled at how my great-grandfather had handmade the beautiful grooves. Such detail! How painstakingly he must have worked on this, carving row after row of fine ridges, and obviously, with such love.

The workman ended up doing some of the repair needed, then hired a violin maker to do the ridges and grooves by hand, so all the trim would match.

When it was finished, they took a soft wax and rubbed it into the wood, so that it had a soft, clean lustre. It was truly a treasure.

There are times when we all need some restoration. It's best to not let just anyone do it! As a friend of mine says, "There is only one of you. so take good care of yourself". Fortunately there is One we can trust for the outcome every time: our heavenly Father.

That is good news.

Be... Still... Know

For everything there is a season. A time to be quiet and a time to speak. Ecclesiastes 3:1-7

I wait quietly before God, for my victory comes from him. Psalm 62:1 (NLT)

First it looked sort of foggy. After the sun burned away the mist, we could see the beautiful hot air balloon. I wondered if it was quiet up there in the basket, under the balloon.

I've not ever been up in one of those, but when I tried paragliding, the noise of the wind currents surprised me. I had totally expected silence.

Quiet. Not an easy thing. A prayer I find myself saying often (maybe too often!) is for my mouth to stay closed at the right times, and not say anything, as well as prayers to say the right thing.

It's difficult for me to be still. Period. I'm a fairly active person. If I'm not up and doing something, I am thinking of what I will do when I do get up and going.

I was reminded, about two weeks after seeing the hot air balloon, about this being quiet thing. We were visiting friends who have a retreat in the North Carolina mountains. As we sat in the very, very silent chapel of QuietReflections, the verse from Psalms 46 came into my mind: "Be still, and know that I am God."

Be. Be still. Then know. Hmm...

Sometimes God speaks loud and clear. This was one of those times.

Thank you Lord, that you care enough about us to get our attention, and speak to us in ways that we can hear you. Help us to hear You today, with the ears of our hearts. In Jesus' name. Amen.

Bitter Root

"See to it that no one misses the grace of God and that no bitter root grows up to cause trouble and defile many." Hebrews 12:15

Finally I couldn't stand looking at it anymore. Every time I went out the door, the plant would catch my eye. And every time it seemed bigger than the last time I looked at it.

The oyster plant is not a weed. It does "volunteer", however, all over the place. It spreads and multiplies in concrete cracks, grass, and just about anywhere. The top sides of the leaves are long, green blades; the undersides are purple. Small white flowers form around the stalk, encased in reddish pouches. They are tough as nails and can root practically from anything; sometimes even a broken leaf.

So I twisted over and reached down to yank it out by the root, but only the top came off in my grip. I reached back in and pulled harder, but still got just a few more leaves. Firmly stuck down in the sandy dirt, squeezed behind a piece of roof tile, it held its ground, literally.

I thought, "If that root stays there, there will be a lot more of these before you know it!"

That's the whole thing about roots. If you get most or all of the plant out, but not the root, you haven't really accomplished anything. It will come back and spread.

I've heard caution about harboring a "bitter root". It is dangerous. I looked up the verses for "bitter root" in the bible, and found two. They certainly are giving me something to ponder. Any way you cut it, it looks like a not-good thing to have a bitter root.

"Make sure there is no man or woman, clan or tribe among you today whose heart turns away from the Lord our God to go and worship the gods of those nations; make sure there is no root among you that produces such bitter poison." Deuteronomy 29:18

Bridges Not Walls

..then make my joy complete by being like-minded, having the same love, being one in spirit and purpose. Philippians 2:2

Hmmmm, I thought. Actually I was thinking a few things, when I opened and read the email that was not-so-nice. It stung for a moment, and for a second I thought about replying with something on about the same par. Then, I had an epiphany moment (fortunately) and thought about how it is better - by far - to build bridges, than walls. It is worth whatever it takes; not to say you have to compromise, in order to build bridges.

Jamie Buckingham, a pastor from Melbourne, FL, and an author who did a lot of ghostwriting, was a firm believer in that. He invested much of his life here on earth, building bridges between charismatic, pentecostal, and evangelical Christians.

The enemy's plan never changes, so it's no big surprise: deceive > divide > destroy, That's right, Satan doesn't just want to hassle us a little bit, or maybe mess up our lives. He wants to take us down, then take us out.

Divisiveness is not of God. God is pro-unity. The last prayer Jesus prayed with his friends, is recorded in the,17th chapter of the book of John. It is a prayer for us:

"I pray also for those who will believe in me through their (the disciples') message, that all of them may be one, Father, just as you are in me and I am in you. May they also be in us so that the world may believe that you have sent me. I have given them the glory that you gave me, that they may be one as we are one: I in them and you in me. May they be brought to complete unity to let the world know that you sent me and have loved them even as you have loved me." - Jesus (John 17:20-23)

Prayer: Lord, please help us to build bridges, not walls. Building bridges. The better way. In Jesus' name. Amen.

Captured

You saw me before I was born. Every day of my life was recorded in your book. Every moment was laid out before a single day had passed. Psalm 139:16 NLT

The rosy sunset began seeping across the sky. I quickly grabbed my new camera, all excited for an opportunity to capture and hold onto the glorious sight.

When I received the camera as a gift last Christmas, it came with an instruction manual. The section on how to best photograph subjects and landscapes, etc., was spelled out in great detail. The thick booklet described how to capture the moment.

Today, at the grocery store, I saw a pre-schooler in the parking lot. She was bent over, completely fascinated by something on the ground. Maybe a bug, or a leaf, or a rock, or a piece of paper. Whatever it was, she was trying, without success, to get her mother's attention to come look at it.

The child was oblivious to the fact that Mom wanted to get in the store and get the grocery shopping done, back home, unpacked, and put away. She did not realize Mom had many other things to do today, She was totally captured by the moment.

God is in every moment we have. How awesome to be so enthralled with the moment. There used to be a phrase, "Stop and smell the roses." Each moment is truly a gift from the Lord.

Today, may I be filled with gratitude, to my Creator, and see the beauty and awe of "the moment".

Carving Your Initials

"The Lord... heals the brokenhearted and binds up their wounds." Psalm 147:2-3

Peggy and Bill invested their lives in others. They worked tirelessly defending children in the court system who had no one else to help them.

One clear, sunny day around noon, their small plane took off from the local airport. Within five minutes, as they were still flying low, the plane took a dive and crashed right onto a major downtown city street. It was a miracle that the plane didn't land on any cars. Yet it was so very sad that this wonderful couple's lives were so suddenly and prematurely snuffed out.

Many years ago, at a renewal retreat weekend, Peggy had left a gift on my pillow. It was a small unfinished wooden heart, like you'd find in craft stores. Printed in a black marker was "SK + JC". Sally Kennedy plus Jesus Christ. Our initials in a heart, signifying that we love each other.

That miniature wooden heart is still on a shelf in my room. I look at if often, and think of the love Peggy had for Jesus, and for others. I think of how my initials and Jesus' are carved in eternity.

Carving initials in a tree scars the outer bark, but the tree survives and the initials are there for the life of the tree. Likewise, when we have cuts, our skin heals. Our bodies are made by God in such a way that they heal when wounded.

Wounds of the heart are more difficult, though. When our memories are scarred, only Jesus can heal them. We may keep growing, yet the scar remains until the Lord heals us.

The good news is that not only is Jesus able to heal, He is more than willing. Praise God for His goodness! He is the one to remember, when it comes to initials being carved on our hearts.

Deeper

"The Lord does not look at the things man looks at. Man looks at the outward appearance, but the Lord looks at the heart." 1 Samuel 16:7

The small Flats boat was whipping along on top of the sea. There was no bouncing; just gliding on the glassy waters. What a glorious day! My husband was at the wheel, and as we entered a shallow area, he slowed to make sure we didn't get stuck in the sandy bottom.

Gazing out, I watched the horizon meet the Gulf. I was lost in God's beauty, when Ben exclaimed, "Look at these flats. Lots of grass." Then, " Here's a nice low profile reef."

I peered over the edge, and sure enough, purple sea fans were clearly visible. As we drifted a bit deeper, we could see some larger fish and some coral that had a little more dimension.

Being a fisherman, Ben knows that looking beyond the surface, you see more. The farther you travel in the ocean, the more you see.

It's good to go deeper in the word of God, too. There is more to be seen; more revelation.

It is good, also, to go deeper with the Lord in prayer and meditation. Going deeper with God, and His word, affords us wisdom in our day to day relationships.

The bible tells us that God looks beyond the surface, that He is looking deeper; He is looking at our hearts.

Determined

"Let us run with perseverance the race marked out for us... let us fix our eyes on Jesus, the author and perfecter of our faith."
Hebrews 12:1-2

It was a hot, cloudless autumn morning. As I was waking up and enjoying a cup of coffee, my attention was drawn to the birdfeeder hanging outside my study. It is a plexiglas tube with a small rimmed saucer underneath, and it is "squirrel proof".

Sitting in the saucer was the most contented squirrel, munching away to his heart's content on the delicious sunflower seeds meant 'specially for cardinals.

The determined squirrel had overcome some obstacles to get from his nest high in the palm fronds to the birdfeeder. Once he'd gotten there, it was no doubt difficult to climb onto the slippery feeding tray. He'd calculated his timing so there were no birds at the feeder; he could have it all to himself without a fight.

He persevered. He was determined. He got his hourishment because he purposed to do it. Today, I must decide and purpose to get the spiritual food I desire - and need - to both stay alive and to grow in my faith.

Prayer: Lord, thank you for the path you have carefully carved out for me in this life. Lord, you know I get tired sometimes and I need your gift of perseverance. Please help me to hang in there. In Jesus' name, Amen.

Drippy and Drizzly

Sounds like the two dwarfs who didn't make the cut for the Disney movie. Drippy and drizzly. That is how it's been for the past 2 days. When you are on vacation, that's the last thing you want: rain. But you know what they say, "can't do much about the weather".

I watched the clouds drip onto the water, making hypnotic little circles that merged into other circles. How the years melted, and I was transported to a place far away.

At a remote spot, at the end of a long dirt road, was the clearing with a pretty spring-fed lake and a sprinkling of cottages; one of which my parents honeymooned in, then later purchased.

I spent summers there as a child. Rustic hardly describes it. Today, I believe camping would be more sophisticated than life at our cottage was back then.

It was the best time of my life. Well, one of the very best, for sure. Life was so simple. We enjoyed reading stories and books; we put together lots of puzzles. Outdoors there were limitless opportunities for creative play and on sunny afternoons, we could swim.

Every summer we would borrow a farm dog, and he'd be our friend for the months we were there. He, my sister, and I had many an adventure in the old rowboat, scouting bullfrogs on lily pads.

Today I am thankful for time to be still, like those days. To just "be", and not "do". I am too often guilty of operating as a "human doing" and not a "human being".

God can really use our drippy, drizzly days, to quiet our minds, minister to our souls, and settle our spirits.

That is good news.

Psalm 46:10 (NIV) Be still, and know that I am God Psalm 55: 6-8 (MSG) Get me out of here on dove wings; I want some peace and quiet. I want a walk in the country. I want a cabin in the woods. I'm desperate for a change from rage and stormy weather. Psalm 4:4 (ASV) Stand in awe, and sin not: Commune with your own heart upon your bed, and be still. Ps 131:2 (NKJV) Surely I have calmed and quieted my soul.

First Comes Love

"We love because He first loved us." 1 John 4:19

Our ice cream cones were cold and creamy, and so delicious. We wiped up the melts and drips, and piled back in my car. Traffic was heavy, requiring my full attention. Jackson started pestering his sister, who was trying, in the nicest way, to ignore him. That didn't work because he kept up the pestering, and starting hitting her knee. She asked him once, twice, and a third time to "Stop it!" He was getting the better of her, but she knew how to get him. She began whispering, "Jackson and Eva, sittin' in a tree, k-i-s-s-i-n-g; first comes love, then comes marriage, then comes Jackson with the baby carriage."

When he started getting mad and turning red, she knew she had him. I remembered the rhyme. In elementary school years we used to recite it while jumping rope.

First comes love. This morning the scripture verse on my calendar was from the fifth chapter of the book of Galatians: "The fruit of the spirit is love, joy, and peace".

I thought, LOVE, joy, and peace. First is love. That is the most important. Without it, can we have the others?

I was mulling this over, and thought that all of these surely must flow from love. There is no joy without love, nor peace without love- both giving and receiving. In fact the Bible says "The entire law is summed up in a single command: "Love your neighbor as yourself." (Galatians 5:14)

Love. The thirteenth chapter of Corinthians is the great "love chapter", quoted often in wedding vows. And First John, chapter 4, is loaded with LOVE stuff, especially verses 7-12 and 16-18).

Yes, the evidence (fruit) in believers' lives is *"love, joy, peace, patience, kindness, goodness, faithfulness, gentleness and self-control." (Galatians 5:22)*

And first comes love.

Forcing the Flower

He has made everything beautiful in its time. Ecclesiastes 3:11

Several days had passed since I bought the beautiful big, plump rose. I cut the stem at an angle, under water (as the directions suggested). Then I placed it in a special bud vase, and set it on my husband's washstand. Ben loves roses, and although this flower didn't have much fragrance, it was lovely to look at.

The flower just wasn't opening like I thought it should.

"I'll help it," I thought. So carefully, I pried the blush color petals open.

Perhaps you have tried to force a flower to open before it is ready. It didn't work for me, that's for sure.

So often I am impatient with how things are going, and I just have to get involved and try to "help" speed up the process. I am an action person, so have always prided myself on not procrastinating; rather taking the bull by the horns and jumping in.

Forcing this flower to open clearly brought home the message to me that, even though it is ok to be an action person, it is also wise to be patient. There is a rhythm, and a time, for everything. My impatience helps nothing!

Thank you , Lord, You make everything beautiful, in Your time.

That is Good News.

❖ *Ecclesiastes 3*

1 There is a time for everything,
and a season for every activity under heaven:
2 a time to be born and a time to die,
a time to plant and a time to uproot,
3 a time to kill and a time to heal,
a time to tear down and a time to build,
4 a time to weep and a time to laugh,
a time to mourn and a time to dance,
5 a time to scatter stones and a time to gather them,
a time to embrace and a time to refrain,
6 a time to search and a time to give up,
a time to keep and a time to throw away,
7 a time to tear and a time to mend,
a time to be silent and a time to speak,
8 a time to love and a time to hate,
a time for war and a time for peace.

Gifts

"If you... know how to give good gifts to your children, how much more will your Father in heaven give good gifts to those who ask him!" Matthew 7:11

Maybe we give gifts according to where we are at the time, rather than where the person is who is receiving the gift.

Last week, I bought the loveliest handkerchief for my sister. It is old-fashioned looking and has her initial on it. I was in a nostalgic and sentimental mood at the time. She's not a very frilly of fluffy person. But she will probably like it, since her favorite sister will be presenting it to her.

This afternoon, I bought my friend some smiley-face pencils for her upcoming birthday. I like them, and although it is a small gift, she will no doubt appreciate the thought behind it.

A long time ago, our Father decided to give us a gift. He picked something He wanted to give us: a bridge back to Him, and the relationship He has always wanted with us   It cost Him a bundle, but He gave us the gift anyway, because that's where He was at, loving us that much.

Lord, thank you that I am your priceless and treasured possession. Thank you for creating me to fellowship with You, the eternal God. Help me, Lord, to understand the deep truth of that. In Jesus' name, Amen.

Handmade

"Then God said, 'Let us make man in our image, in our likeness... So God created man in his own image.'" Genesis 1:26-27

Maybe it sounds corny, but I like handmade presents best. Not to say that I don't like silver and sparkly, but a handmade gift is a treasured bit of the gift-giver.

This past Christmas I received a card from Taylor, my eleven-year-old granddaughter. It was special because she thought of it, she created it with love, customized it just for me, and gave it to me. Another special present was a double picture frame, with 2 photos in it, from my sister. The old black and white on the left is the two of us when were were really young. On the right is a photo of us taken on my recent birthday. It's a special gift, handmade with love, and holding countless memories.

Do you know that we, too, are handmade gifts? We are gifts to the world, and to each other. God made us, and we know that everything we see was made by Him.

Handmade gifts are the best gifts- sharing the heart and soul of the giver.

Hidden

"For... your life is now hidden with Christ in God." Colossians 3:3

A perfect day for a mid-morning walk, before the heat of the day settled in like a damp blanket.

As my husband rounded the bend, he asked, "Did you see that squirrel?" No, I hadn't. I peered into the woods. Still couldn't see it.

"He's right there", Ben said.

I was determined to see it. As I kept scanning, I stepped closer. There it was, amazingly camouflaged. Ha! "No wonder I didn't see it", I thought. It blended right into the sticks and brushy leaves.

That little animal was so perfectly hidden. Reminded me of the verse in the Bible where it talks about us being hidden in Christ. I thought again of how it's all about Him, not me/us.

Today, Lord, let me be hidden in You, so that what is visible is you and not me.

Holding Onto the "B"

" The Lord is the one who goes ahead of you; He will be with you He will not fail you or forsake you. Do not fear or be dismayed." Deuteronomy 31:8

Three-year-old Tommy, whose new hat was nearly half the size of him, had never been this close to a horse before. He was so excited to get to it! We were on a family vacation, and as I watched Tommy struggling to reach through the fence and pat the horse's nose, I was nodding and shaking my head at the same time.

He was holding his "b" In his left hand, the blankie that went everywhere with him, even on the airplane and out to see the horses. The only problem was that he couldn't quite negotiate getting his hand through the fence hole without dropping the "b". And he wasn't about to drop the "b".

I couldn't help but think of how many times there is something good out there, I want to move forward, take the next step, yet I want to hold on to the security of the past. I just can't let go of something for fear of how I would be able to manage without it. Kind of reminds me of a story I heard once about a daddy and his young daughter who had a strand of pink plastic pearls.

God asks us to grow in our Christian walk. We don't have to do it alone; in fact we can't. 1 Peter 2-3 says," Like newborn babies, crave pure spiritual milk, so that by it you may grow up in your salvation, now that you have tasted that the Lord is good." The "meat", more of God, is a blessing,

Our "b's" are wonderful for a season, then comes a time we no longer have to hold onto them. May we have the courage and grace to let go and trust our Heavenly Father to take care of us in the next step He has for us. He is already there anyway;

I had a friend that used to put it this way, "you can't go anywhere that God is not already there." That is good news.

Hovercraft

"Now the earth was formless and empty, darkness was over the surface of the deep, and the Spirit of God was hovering over the waters. And God said, "Let there be light," and there was light. God saw that the light was good." Genesis 1:2-4

Hovercraft; kind of a funny word. Many years ago we had an opportunity to take a ride on a hovercraft. I thought we were getting onto a ferry to cross a body of water. We drove our cars onto it, as if driving onto a large ferry boat.

Once underway, the vessel sort of inflated under us, and we went roaring off across the sea. I learned that, in principle, it's a craft that skims over the water (or land) on a cushion of air created by jet engines. It was quite an experience.

Not long ago I was studying the first chapter, in the first book, of the Bible, Genesis. "In the beginning God." In Genesis 1 it says the Spirit of God hovered over the waters; then God spoke, and something happened. A creative miracle; something GOOD.

Luke 1:35, says, "The angel answered, The Holy Spirit will come upon you, the power of the Highest hover over you; Therefore, the child you bring to birth will be called Holy, Son of God." (The Message)

I believe the Holy Spirit hovers today, before something happens (something good). A good prayer might be, "Hover over us, Holy Spirit. We can then look with expectation to whatever good thing You are going to do. In Jesus' mighty name Amen."

How Vast

How precious to (or concerning) me are your thoughts, O God!
How vast is the sum of them! Were I to count them, they would
outnumber the grains of sand. Psalm 139:17-18

Each year my husband and I try to get out to the Rockies. We
love the drier air, and those majestic mountains. In September,
the two peaks called "Maroon Bells", are magnificent. The aspen
trees, which cover and coat the hillsides, turn quickly from a
lush green to a golden yellow.

It looked like a giant head of broccoli gone to seed. My eyes
were seeing it, while my mind iwas trying to figure how tall just
one of those trees were.

It was impossible to get my mind around the huge gigantic
numbers of trees it takes to make up that mountainside view. All
I could think of, as I gazed on this incredible site last year, was:
how vast. How vast!!

The verse came to my mind from the Bible, about how vast are
the sum of God's thoughts..towards me. Some translations even
say "concerning" me.

Wow. Something else I will never fathom. That's OK, though,
because God is God. And I'm not. I am ever-grateful and ever-
thankful our heavenly Father, for the beauty He puts in our
world, and for His thoughts towards His children.

"Bless the Lord, oh my soul, and all that is within me, bless His
holy name."

Keys in the Snow

"Let us not become weary in doing good, for at the proper time we will reap a harvest if we do not give up."   Galatians 6:9

My husband and I had a real treat recently when our friend, Michele, invited us to spend a few days in their home in the mountains. Ben was thrilled to have an opportunity to get out his skis and head for the slopes. I, too, so much enjoyed the R & R in a place so very different from our home in south Florida.

Off the back wood deck of the house, there was a large iron antique key. It occurred to me that keys in the snow are like seeds buried underground in winter; some big, some smaller. The seeds aren't just lying there doing nothing. They are building energy, while resting, to germinate and sprout. And when the inactivity of a winter season is over, spring gets underway. Pretty soon, what's going on is visible to OUR eyes. A tiny green blade pokes through, and we're on the way.

The dream God has crafted just for you might be your seed. Perhaps it is still buried deep underneath a thick layer of snow. The blanket of insulation can protect it while preparation is happening. God gave you the dream. He takes care to let nothing happen to it.

Hopefully, I can remember not to throw in the towel, but to hang in there. There's a plan for those "keys" in the snow. Really.

Lightning Strikes

"Then he said to the man, 'Stretch out your hand.' So he stretched it out and it was completely restored, just as sound as the other." Matthew 12:13

It stood as tall and as straight as all the other trees in the glen. Clearly visible, right down the front of the trunk was a deep mark. Lightning had struck the tree at some point and slashed its exterior, gouging out a path.

Lightning is usually lethal. It didn't kill this tree, however, nor did it cause the tree to catch fire and burn up. The tree survived the strike, the wound healed, and the scar is the only evidence remaining that it suffered a near death experience. Not only did it survive, the tree is doing great! It is healthy and leafy. It stands tall and stately in the woods by the hiking trail for many to enjoy.

In our journeys, chances are we have been, or will be, struck by "unfriendly fire". From debilitating diseases to personal and relationship crises, many things can "hit" us in life. If we hold on to the Rock, and we stay rooted and grounded in Christ, we can - and will - survive. We might be scarred, but that doesn't mean we aren't whole, healed, and happy again.

Lightning does strike, and God does heal and restore. That is good news.

Little Springs

To each one the manifestation of the Spirit is given for the common good. All these are the work of one and the same Spirit, and he gives them to each one, just as he determines. The body is a unit, though it is made up of many parts; and though all its parts are many, they form one body. 1 Corinthians 12:7,11-12

I almost missed it. The ground looked soggy, the trail puddly. And muddy. On closer look, a little spring was coming from under a rock to the right of the trail.

One little spring. Enough water to give drink to animals, birds. As it meandered across the road, and downhill on the massive mountain, it would join other little springs.

The little springs would merge and eventually flow together into one mighty river at the base of the mountain. Together they would make beautiful music as one, as they rolled through the floor of the mountain valley.

Little springs. Like different gifts and talents, I thought. Individually they are wonderful, and have a purpose. Sort of like musical instruments. So great individually. Together, though, they create bands, and songs; orchestras, and symphonies.

God gives the gifts as He sees fit. And every believer is guaranteed one or more. He alone knows what beautiful music they will make together for us, as well as for others.

That is good news!

Magic Mirror

"Now we see but a poor reflection as in a mirror; then we shall see face to face. Now I know in part; then I shall know fully, even as I am fully known." 1 Corinthians 13:12

"Mirror, mirror on the wall, who is the fairest of them all?"

In the Disney children's classic, the magic mirror always told the wicked queen that she was the fairest in the land. Until Snow White, that is. Then the magic mirror became a reflection of truth. What if we had a magic mirror like that? It might reveal things about us we'd rather not see, and face up to. Perhaps we would view things as they really are, not as we want them to be.

I've a long list of questions to ask in heaven. I suspect many others do, too. One day the questions will be answered. We will understand.

Meantime, while on this earth, we can be a mirror, and "magically" supernaturally reflect the love of God.

St. Paul says, in 2 Corinthians 3:18, *"And all of us, as with unveiled face, [because we] continued to behold [in the Word of God] as in a mirror the glory of the Lord, are constantly being transfigured into His very own image in ever increasing splendor and from one degree of glory to another; [for this comes] from the Lord [Who is] the Spirit. " (AMP)*

Lord, today, may others see Your kindness and Love, mirrored in me, through Holy Spirit. In Jesus' name. Amen.

Morning Glory

"In the morning, oh Lord, you hear my voice; in the morning I lay my requests before you and wait in expectation." Psalm 5:3

Some people seem to be born "morning people", while others are not. I'm in the "not" group. So even though I kept meaning to walk over and take a photo of the morning glory vines nearby, it was lunchtime before I got there.

I had seen them earlier, from the car, and they were in full color array. Vibrant periwinkle blue, on bright green leaves, stretched from the planter box downstairs all the way up to the second story.

In the heat of mid-day, the vines were still there, but the flowers had closed. The glory of these lovely flowers was reserved for the morning.

The book of Psalms has always been a source of inspiration and comfort to me. Something in my spirit and soul begins to calm down and become serene when I read the words David, penned so long ago.

I thought about what the bible says in the psalms about praying in the morning. Of course you can pray anytime, which is a good thing to do. But there is something about praying in the morning, even before getting out of bed, that is special.

This timeless confession, by David, the *"man after God's own heart" (Acts 13:22, 1 Samuel 13:14), is good for me to heed, each and every morning: "In the morning, oh Lord, you hear my voice; in the morning I lay my requests before you and wait in expectation."*

New Growth

"He has made everything beautiful in its time." Ecclesiastes
3:11

It is springtime here in south Florida where we live. There are
signs of new growth all about. This morning while walking I
noticed all the light coloring of the season. The grass and all the
varied trees are in their glorious pastel shades of green. It is so
pretty, yet not nearly as eye-catching and dramatic as darker,
brighter colors of more mature growth in full bloom.

Similarly, in our Christian walks, we are more pale and stand out
less in earlier parts of our journeys. As we grow and mature and
"hang out" with Jesus, we take on deeper, richer, more brilliant
hues of the attributes of Jesus himself. We become easier to
spot; singled out out more quickly.

God grows us all beautiful in His time. That's good news.
Prayer: Thank you, Lord, that I am a new creation in Christ, that
the old is gone and the new is here. Thank you for growing me
into the likeness of Christ. In Jesus' name, Amen.

Pockets

"See, I have engraved you on the palms of my hands." Isaiah 49:16

While visiting a friend in Vermont this past summer, she gifted me with a cool present: a green and white sweatshirt with "Ireland" printed on the front. And it had pockets; two of them!

I love pockets, and I'd never seen them in sweatshirts before. When clothes shopping, I think twice about purchasing pants that have no pockets. I like aprons with pockets, and terry cloth bathrobes that have roomy pockets. They are so handy for everything. There is always something that can be put in the pockets.

When one of our sons was young, he had a miniature hamster. He would carry the hampster around in his shirt pocket and it was the cutest thing to see Butterball's tiny little nose and twitching whiskers peeking over the top.

Sometimes I take our grandkids on treasure hunt walks. All the interesting and cool things we find, like rocks or snail shells, go into our pockets.

An old white bunny with red eyes lives on the chair in my bedroom. She has floppy pink satin-lined ears, and behind her clasped front paws is a secret pocket. Over the years it has held many different items, all carefully hidden there.

The bible says that we are carried around in the palm of God's hand. I like to think we're in His pocket; the one that's real close to His heart.

Yes, pockets can indeed hold priceless treasures.

Real or Fake

"For false Christs and false prophets will appear and perform signs and miracles to deceive the elect - if that were possible."
Mark 13:22, Matthew 24:24

My sister is quite a yard nut. She loves more than anything to be out in her yard, digging in the dirt, trimming, weeding, planting, and transplanting. Poison ivy gets her if she isn't really careful, but several bouts haven't stopped her from her favorite pastime.

Last week we were visiting Marion and her husband, and she couldn't wait to walk me around outside. She excitedly showed me this, that and the other (names I can never remember). Some flowers caught my eye; I remarked, "Oh! Irises. I love irises. They are just beautiful!" She laughed and said, "Oh, only the top ones are real. I just stuck the other ones in there. They're fake!"

They all looked real to me. So I got a little closer; they still all looked about the same. I went up really close to inspect, and touched the petals. Sure enough, the pinkish ones were artificial; the purple on top, genuine.

Real, fake. Sometimes it is hard to tell which is which. I have been fooled by imitation jewels, like cubic zirconia, which resemble diamonds. The difference is just short of polar, but I couldn't tell.

In the Bible, there's a warning: He (Jesus) replied: *"Watch out that you are not deceived. For many will come in my name, claiming, 'I am he,' and, 'The time is near.' Do not follow them. (Luke 21:8*

Real, fake. How can you tell which is which?. When it comes to spiritual things, we can rely on the Holy Spirit, who witnesses to the Truth, which always lines up with the Word of God.

"But when he, the Spirit of truth, comes, he will guide you into all truth." (the words of Jesus, John 16:13)

Real or fake; the Lord can tell us. That is good news.

The Fine Print

"Have faith in God... believe... and when you stand praying... "
Mark 11:24-25

There it was, at the very bottom of the document, in noticably smaller size print: the disclaimer. Have you ever noticed these sections at the end of a contract or agreement? I'm reminded of the saying, "Read the fine print before signing on the dotted line."

That little part stuck on at the end might sometimes be called "the catch". When things seem too good to be true, they usually are. We tend to ask, "What's the catch?"

There is an amazing promise in the bible that might sound too good to be true. About a week before Jesus was killed and came back to life, He was talking with His close friends. He said that if you believe, you can have anything you ask for in prayer. (Mark 11:24)

Could it be that easy? Perhaps the very next sentence is the fine print. Practically in the same breath, Jesus continues, essentially saying that we have to forgive anyone we hold a grudge against first. That could even be ourselves.

The fine print of forgiveness is a key to unlocking and releasing God's promises. Yes, it's always good ro read the fine print.

Tightly Wrapped

"... and let him go." John 11:44

There's been a food fad around for awhile now called 'wraps'. Veggie wraps, ham and cheese wrap, chicken Caesar wrap; you name it. 'Tightly wrapped' is a phrase sometimes used for people who are high strung; those who might need to lighten up or "get a life". Lazarus was a guy who was tightly wrapped. Not in a nervous angst but literally "wrapped". The bible tells the story (John 11).

Lazarus was one of Jesus' best friends; someone He could hang out with, relax, have dinner with, talk things over with. Apparently Jesus often spend the night with Lazarus and his sisters whenever He went to Jerusalem.

Anyway, Lazarus died. When Jesus arrived at Bethany, not far from Jerusalem, He went to the tomb with Mary, Martha, and the others. He was moved to tears, and after praying to His Father, He called in a loud voice, "Lazarus, come out!"

The dead man came out, with all the burial cloths on, his hands and feet wrapped with strips of linen, and a cloth around his face. Then the bible says, '"Jesus said to them, 'Take off the grave clothes and let him go'."

Jesus raised Lazarus from the dead and gave him life. Yet He told the people to rip off and unravel those grave clothes, so that Lazarus could freely move on.

Jesus is still in the business of saving lives, calling us to leave a life that leads to spiritual death, and urging us to embrace a spiritual resurrection and new life by believing in Him. Then, sometimes, He says to us: "Loose him/her, and let him go".

This is where forgiveness can come in. We can keep others tied up with unforgiveness. They can have new life in Christ, be 'born-again', and yet be bound up unless we forgive and turn them loose.

The gospels all speak about forgiving others as we have been forgiven. It is a mandate that we make the decision to choose to forgive, whether we feel like it or not. Surely we don't want to be 'tightly wrapped'; it is our privilege, and responsibility, to allow our brothers and sisters the same freedom.

Too Tight Shoes

"Come, follow me," Jesus said Matthew 4:19

My husband hates to go shopping. Especially clothes shopping. At the mall. But the sneakers he'd had for a long time had seen their day. He decided to bite the bullet and go for it, make the dreaded trip to the store and get some new sneakers for our trip.

Oh boy! The weather was sooo gorgeous. We couldn't wait to get on our walking shoes and get going. Not too far into the hike, Ben said "You know, these shoes are kind of bothering me! They feel sort of tight or something."

We pressed on. The sky was so clear, the air so cool, the trees so deep green that there was little thought given to the shoes again.

Until we got back to where we were staying. He peeled off the new shoes and socks, to discover not only an ugly blister rubbed on his heel, but also a bone bruise by his large toe.

My husband's shoes were too small. He only wore them one day. Not even one whole day. The injury and bruising he sustained took all week to heal. It definitely curtailed activity. We did try hiking again, and he wore some other shoes which were not at all fit for the job.

In the sixth chapter of Ephesians, Paul tells us how to put on the armor of God. He says "wear shoes that are able to speed you on as you preach the Good News of peace with God". Other versions say "sandals of peace".

If I am not walking in peace, I am in too small. too tight shoes. Prayer: Lord, please help me choose the right shoes today, the best shoes for this day, that I might follow in Your foot steps. Thank you, Lord. Amen.

Under the Wallpaper

"For you were once darkness, but now you are light in the Lord. Live as children of light." Ephesians 5:8

The only telltale sign anything was wrong with the wallpaper in the bathroom, was that it was curling up at the bottom corner. It looked pretty good, but underneath, we discovered black mold. The yucky stuff had to have been growing there a long time in order to get that bad. We finally determined that it had come from a hairline crack in the wall- a small water leak that had gone undetected until the paper was in this state.

Underneath the wallpaper, the damage was so extensive that even some of the plaster was chunking off. The diagnosis was bad; the cure, worse: we had to take all the paper off, sand the wall, replaster, sand some more, and paint. Amazing how it could look so good on the outside and be so disintegrated and deteriorated on the inside.

That is true of us, too. There have been times in my life when I looked pretty good on the outside, but what was going on under the exterior was far different.

Sometimes things have to grow and fester for a long time. Eventually, when they get bad enough, things begin to change on the outside. Little habits, a little unforgiveness held onto, or a little dishonesty here or there. Small things build and grow, when they're not cleared up and being resolved.

Often this can lead to attitude, people, or business problems, to say nothing of what isn't happening in the relationship with our Father God who desperately desires intimacy with us.

I have been examining the wall paper in other spots. I'm also checking the paper in another room of the house. I was reminded, through all of this, that it would be a good idea to check under the "wallpaper" of my skin, to look into my heart and see if there are any little moldy things growing there. Better to take care of problems early on before the repair is major.

Prayer: Thank you Lord for Your faithfulness, that You are always faithful, even in times that I am not. Today Lord, please bring to light and expose anything in my life that needs attention; anything that is not of You. In Jesus' name, amen.

Upload, Download

"If any of you lacks wisdom, he should ask God, who gives generously to all without finding fault, and it will be given to him." James 1:5

For a non-techie type person such as myself, all the computer lingo is pretty foreign sounding. I think I finally can distinguish between "download" and "upload". I only really got the hang of that by default. Here's my definition of download: something comes in from somewhere in cyber space that contains data. I'm sure that is nowhere near correct, but it helps me differentiate.

Recently I thought about how we get downloads from God all the time. They come primarily from His Word, the Bible; then from other books, other Christians, and circumstances.

This brought to mind the question about uploads. Those would be our prayers. And just as the experts say no email is ever really lost or trashed, none of our prayers ever get lost or erased either.

In Revelations 5 we read about a scene in the throne room of God: " Each one had a harp and they were holding golden bowls full of incense, which are the prayers of the saints."

Right now I need some supernatural wisdom. I need the mind of Christ, God's insight and direction. I'm so thankful that I can go to Him in prayer, lay everything out before Him, and ask for what I need at the moment. And I am so thankful that He doesn't shut me out or shut me down. He knows the cries of our hearts; He listens, and He answers.

Upload: our prayers; download: from the Lord.

That is good news.

What's In a Name?

God gave him the name above all other names. Philippians 2:9

"Sticks and stones may hurt my bones, but names can never hurt me."

Or can they? And if names can be hurtful, can they be helpful? Healing?

In some countries, people were named after their parents. For example, if you were Ben's son, you might be called Benson. Or Martin's son, Martinson. One of Jesus' names was Jesus Bar Joseph, Jesus son of Joseph.

The names used in the Bible often have spiritual significance and are descriptive of those persons. The name Isaac meant 'laughter', Moses drawn out of water, Sarah - 'princess', Eve 'life', David beloved. God has many names. A couple are Jehovah Jireh (the Lord who provides, Gen.22:14), and Jehovah Rohi (the Lord is my Shepherd, Ps. 23:1)

Do our names define us?

As believers, we can claim the names: redeemed, adopted, saved, set free, holy, set aside, healed, whole, chosen, sent, and Christian, follower of Christ.

I am thankful today, that whatever my given name, or how others have defined me, I am a child of the King!

Worn Lightly

"Cast all your anxiety on him because he cares for you." 1 Peter 5:7 (NIV)

Tiny puffs of feathery snow, silently, gently floated down from heaven to earth. What a glorious sight it was. It was thrilling to sit that morning and watch the awesome and magnificent sight of the late snowfall. I thought about how beautiful God made the world for us.

Just in front of the window was a large evergreen bough. I found it interesting that, as the snow continued to fall and mound up on the branch, it never did cause it to dip or bend. The evergreen was wearing it's new "burden" lightly, as 'not of the world'.

There's a place in the Bible where Jesus talks about this; He says to take His yoke upon you, which is light, and easy, rather than the heaviness of the world. *("Take my yoke upon you and learn from me, for I am gentle and humble in heart, and you will find rest for your souls. For my yoke is easy and my burden is light." Matthew 11)*

We don't have to carry around heavy things, nor carry the world on our shoulders. We weren't meant to have stooped, sagging shoulders from bearing heavy cares and worries.

In 1st Peter 5, it says, *"Casting the whole of your care [all your anxieties, all your worries, all your concerns, once and for all] on Him, for He cares for you affectionately and cares about you watchfully.". (AMP)*

We can wear world as a garment of light, not as a cloak that suffocates and strangles. How wonderful that Jesus did and does that for us.

That is very good news.

Section II

God has said, *"Never will I leave you;*
never will I forsake you." Hebrews 13:5

Alllll Aboard!

"... you will sing as on the night you celebrate a holy festival; your hearts will rejoice." Isaiah 30:29

We were in the midst of a tropical depression. That's when lots of gray, soggy clouds sit there and don't go anywhere. Day after day the rains kept coming. When we have flash floods, the rain waters steadily rise creating deep, dangerous puddles in driveways and streets.

In other parts of the country, there had been heavy rains and flooding. Rivers would swell. Whole towns were covered with water when the quickly rising waters spilled over the banks. Many homes and possessions were destroyed and washed away.

Troubles have a way of piling up and flooding our lives when they are not dealt with. Ordinary day-in, day-out things get to be more of a hassle than when it's business-as-usual. Life looks cloudy and gray, then dark, and the 'waters' begin to rise. We can't see a light at the end of the tunnel. No sun, no birds chirping. Anxiety edges in. It is a sin to worry. Yet sometimes it is hard for my head to get that through to my heart, especially in the middle of a personal 'tropical depression'.

As it takes time for the ground to absorb the extra water during bouts of flash floods, so it takes time for our troubles to be resolved and dissipate. Here's some good news. The ark floated on the rising waters, and we can too.

According to tradition, Noah's Ark landed on Mr. Ararat, one of the highest mountain peaks in the world. When the flood waters are rising all around you, check to make sure you're on board with the Lord, on His "ark". Not only will you not be swept away and drowned; you will land on higher ground.

Alllll Aboard!

Back Covers

" ....be alert and always keep on praying for all the saints."
Ephesians 6:18

There's a popular expression, 'He's an open book.' If people were books, the back covers would be just as important, or more so, than the front covers.

The front cover provides minimal information: title and author and something nice, like a photo or graphic design. The back cover usually contains lots of information: endorsements, an author blurb, what the book is about and why you should buy it and read it.

Often we are assaulted, emotionally or spiritually, in our most vulnerable places. Coming up from behind, attacking from the back, is the sneaky way to do it. Another expression comes to mind: 'stabbed in the back'.

It is wonderful and wise to daily "put on the armor of God", as we are instructed by St. Paul in the bible (Ephesians, sixth chapter). However even with the breastplate, which covers all our shoulder area and front, protecting some vital organs, our backs are still bared.

Picture a circle of people, all facing forward, side by side. Now picture the same circle as each person turns to the right. This is how we ourselves, can be the protection for another's back attacks. We can cover each other's backs by blanketing them with prayer.

Intercession for another person couldn't be easier: 'Lord, please bless ____ ." These prayers of the saints are so important that they are referred to as the incense that fills the golden bowls in the throne room of God (Rev. 5:8).

Thank the Lord, He has provided human back covers: none other than the saints - who just happen to be us.

Clipping and Snipping

"He cuts off every branch in me that bears no fruit, while every branch that does bear fruit he prunes so that it will be even more fruitful." John 15:2

Last fall we had two devastating hurricanes just three weeks apart. At our home, the first storm ripped off the nails and wire cords that held the thick bouganvilla vine into the concrete. When we were able to return home, we found the entire enormous plant down on the concrete.

My husband got a chain saw to begin the cleanup work. We had huge piles of tree limbs, spindly branches and gnarly trunks; more than twenty-five years' worth. What remained were little stumps. Literally, they looked like dead sticks that were just stuck in the ground.

We went out of town after that, and when we came back, did we have a surprise! Just two weeks to the day that my husband had cut it all down, it was loaded with new growth; beautiful thick green leaves, and long sturdy branches.

I finally understood the story about "pruning" found in the bible. (John 15). I never had really understood it until I witnessed it firsthand with our vine.

It seems Jesus spoke so often in agricultural terms. The people must have understood stories that related to trees, plants, seeds, and growing conditions. These probably made perfect sense to them.

You know what they say, you have to experience something to understand it. I guess that is the gift that God gave me through the loss of this bouganvilla vine. I am grateful for that, and for the implications of the story that are now brought to light for me.

I fully expect the vine to bud any day now. I also expect a bumper crop of magnificent fuschia colored flowers. In the future, when I experience clipping, snipping, and chopping - aka pruning - at the hand of the Master gardener, I will remember this principle: cutting back produces more. It works. Thank you, Lord

Dancing on the Mountain

"You will go out in joy and be led forth in peace; the mountains and hills will burst into song before you, and all the trees of the field will clap their hands." Isaiah 55:12

"The trees of the field will clap their hands". I like that song from the psalms, but have always thought the words were sort of stupid. Until that day on the top of the mountain, on a grassy plateau overlooking valleys, mountain peaks, and somewhere down there- rivers and towns. The alpine meadow was strewn with wildflowers and blanketed with patches of purple lupine, yellow and orange paintbrush, and ivory milkweed.

Reminiscent of the Sermon on the Mount and the Beatitudes, we were sitting around listening to a man teach. That's when I noticed that the tall grass was dancing and waving in the breeze, and the blue spruce was swaying with its branches moving and "clapping".

The pastor waved his arm widely, and said, "If God can do all this (panorama) with dirt, think of what He can do with us."

Yes, think!

Decision and Direction

"If any of you lacks wisdom, he should ask God, who gives generously to all without finding fault, and it will be given to him." James 1:5

and: *"I know, O LORD, that a man's life is not his own; it is not for man to direct his steps." Jeremiah 10:23*

While out for a morning walk today, I turned a corner and saw a white cowbird, similar to a small heron, right in the middle of where two streets intersected. He was quietly standing still, as if trying to decide which way to go. He wasn't ruffled by my presence and nearly let me walk right up to him. He was in his own world for the moment.

How often I stand at the crossroads of a decision, and if I would come out of my own little world of thoughts and look to the Lord for direction, things would go so much more smoothly.

Prayer: Thank you, Father, that you always have a direction in which for us to go, and that you are always so willing to reveal it to us when we ask. Lord, I praise you that you really do order the steps of a righteous person. Thank you that I am righteous in Your eyes, because of the shed blood of Jesus. Glory to you, oh Lord. Amen!

Determined

"Let us run with perseverance the race marked out for us... let us fix our eyes on Jesus, the author and perfecter of our faith."
Hebrews 12:1-2

It was a hot, cloudless autumn morning. As I was waking up, enjoying a cup of coffee, my attention was drawn to the birdfeeder hanging outside my study. It is a plexiglas tube with a small rimmed saucer underneath, and it is "squirrel proof".

Sitting in the saucer was the most contented squirrel, munching away to his heart's content on the delicious sunflower seeds meant 'specially for cardinals.

The determined squirrel had overcome some obstacles to get from his nest high in the palm fronds to the birdfeeder. Once he'd gotten there, it was no doubt difficult to climb onto the slippery feeding tray. He'd calculated his timing so there were no birds at the feeder; he could have it all to himself without a fight.

He persevered. He was determined. He got his nourishment because he purposed to do it. Today, I must decide and purpose to get the spiritual food I desire and need to both stay alive and to grow in my faith.

Prayer: Lord, thank you for the path you have carefully carved out for me in this life. Lord, you know I get tired sometimes and I need your gift of perseverance. Please help me to hang in there. In Jesus' name, Amen.

Drought Survival

"He is like a tree planted by streams of water whose leaf does not wither." Psalm 1:3

In our back yard, there is a spot where red and pink Pentas are planted. These flowers are hardy, and do well in our tropical heat. They are colorful, and are butterfly attractors as well.

Flash floods occasionally soak the Pentas. These plants are resilient, however, and after the soggy, drippy leaves dry out, the flowers bloom brilliantly.

More of a problem than too much water, is too little water. We might go for days, or weeks with no rain; sometimes with scorching sun beating down. They can look kind of pitiful, definitely dried up, with the flowers faded or gone entirely. Yet these plants always bounce back. A bit of rain, a little shade, and they are good-to-go again.

Some plants are created to withstand drought. Are we? In the first book of Psalms, in the Bible, this very thing is addressed. The amplilfied version says it this way:

"Blessed, happy, fortunate, prosperous, and enviable is the man who walks and lives not in the counsel of the ungodly, following their advice, their plans and purposes, ... but his delight and desire are in the precepts, the instructions, the teachings of God; he habitually meditates, ponders and studies by day and by night. And he shall be like a tree firmly planted and tended by the streams of water, ready to bring forth its fruit in its season; its leaf also shall not fade or wither; and everything he does shall prosper and come to maturity."

We may not be as naturally sturdy as Pentas. Yet if we stay near the River of God, and are continually soaked and watered in His

Word, we will not only be able to just make it through droughts, we will flourish in spite of them.

That's good news.

Freedom

"It is for freedom that we have been set free."   *Galatians 5:1*

Freedom is free, but it costs a lot. In our country, we live free today, and by the grace of God it is freely available to us. Yet it carries great cost. The price has been, and continues to be, countless numbers of lives. For over two centuries, men and women have sacrificed their lives and died in many wars, so that we might live in freedom here in the United States of America.

The greatest of all truth is not a saying, thought, or idea. The greatest truth is a person. Jesus said, "I am... truth" (John 14:6).

Knowing Jesus is knowing truth. Knowing Him is what really sets us free. This is the most profound and truest freedom. The cost could hardly have been higher: God's only son.

Lord, we can never thank You enough. This freedom, because of the price you paid, is our very life. Today let me honor Your sacrifice and accept the greatest freedom.

He's a Keeper

"How blessed the hearers and keepers of...all the words written in this book!" Revelations 1:3

With strains of Auld Lang Syne ringing in the air, I was thinking of which things to change, which things to keep, and which to get rid of in the new year. My husband keeps things for a long time; he saves coats and favorite shirts. He's not a pack rat, but he knows which things he likes and tends to hold onto them.

One thing he, my sons and grandsons, all enjoy doing is fishing. Ben has mentioned that fishing rules have become more stringent. He has to sometimes check and see if a fish is a "keeper". Apparently, fines are heavy for keeping a fish that is undersized, or for keeping too many over the quota for the day's catch.

Isn't that just how God is with His kids? He not only loves us; He also likes us. He knows what He likes, and He holds onto them. It's a good thing for us that there is no quota, and no limit.

Indeed, God is a "keeper". He knows what He likes, and keeps them for a long time: forever. That is good news.

Headwaters

"Whoever believes in me... streams of living water will flow from within him." John 7:38

The mighty Roaring Fork River is headquartered in the Colorado Rocky Mountain range along the Continental Divide. The headwaters of that powerful river are deceiving. Up where the river begins, a narrow, calm stream barely leaks out of the mountain. It meanders and wanders, eventually picking up speed and strength as it continues on its journey.

God promised that rivers of living water would flow out of us believers. At the headwaters, the stream may be faint, maybe just a trickle. However, as the water keeps moving, it picks up momentum from and through others, our brothers and sisters. A mighty, roaring river emerges.

You can trust that The River will keep on flowing, growing and gaining momentum for the glory of God.

In a Hurry

"There is a time for everything, and a season for every activity under heaven." Ecclesiastes 3:1

Things can change in a hurry. On Labor Day, the skinny white-trunked aspen trees were very green due to a long wet summer season. Three days later, they were tinged with yellow. In less than a week, they were solid gold. What a majestic sight!

Maybe you or someone you know is in a not-so-great place, and can't see the light at the end of the tunnel. It seems to go on forever, as if it's never going to change.

Change it will, though. Everything has a season. Nothing is forever, except the love of God. The bible tells us, in the book of Psalms, that the love of the Lord endures forever.

While waiting for things to change, reading the Psalms can give us comfort and assuredness that there is a God who loves us and does have a good plan for our lives.

Never give up! It's true that it's always darkest just before dawn. Hang in, and hold on to the Lord. We may get in a rush, but when everything is ready, things will change, and probably in a hurry.

Prayer: Lord, Your ways are not like my ways, and your timing is not like mine. Please increase my trust in You, Lord. I know that Your timing really is perfect. Thank you, Father. In Jesus' name, Amen.

Inside Out

"He is like a tree planted by streams of water, which yields its fruit in season and whose leaf does not wither. Whatever he does prospers." Psalm 1:3

My husband and I were hiking in the magnificent mountains of Colorado. I was mesmerized by the grandeur and beauty all around. I noticed some huge old pines growing out of a big rocky surface. Up toward the tops were pine cones shaped like acorns. I'm no horticulturist, but I know acorns come from oak, not pine trees. So I took a closer look.

The small cones had been cone-shaped, but were turned nearly inside out. The bottoms were there, but the tops were bare and pointed, like bulbs.

I learned that what happens is that the cones are shaped as usual when they first appear. Once the seeds inside are dispersed, they look like these did.

Do you ever practice "seed faith"? Or sow good seed, then feel exhausted and worn out? It is okay to let the Lord "sow seeds" through us, and turn us inside-out. During these times, it's good to remember that we still have our solid base. God IS our steady, strong tree.

Prayer: Lord, thank you that You are my rock; my steady and firm foundation. No matter how the winds of adversity might blow, I praise You that I am still anchored solidly in You. In Jesus' name, Amen.

Is Mother Goose Dead?

"For the word of God is living and active." Hebrews 4:12

The question of the morning was, "Is Mother Goose dead?" My daughter was driving her five-year-old daughter to pre-school. That query was followed up by, "Is she in the cemetery we just passed? Will she be in heaven?" I was laughing as I told her that I couldn't wait to hear her answers.

The "Mother Goose Nursery Rhymes" were first in print in England by the late 1700s. Many of them were politically oriented and veiled as children's poetry. They are around today, and many of us can, no doubt, quote them from memory. I still have the book my mom read to me as a child.

Did you know that the most widely read book in the world isn't nursery rhymes or Aesop's fables, but the Bible? What a wonderful thing that the author of that book is not dead! Although the actual persons who penned it have died, God, who inspired the Bible authors, is very much alive.

The Bible is often called the "Living Word" because it is timeless. The scriptures were applicable and true when they were written down, and they still are applicable and true today. In fact, it is amazing how precisely they relate to our lives today!

Try it: http://www.biblegateway.com

It will make a believer out of you.

It's Who You Know

"... they will all know me, from the least of them to the greatest."
Hebrews 8:11

Yesterday my daughter was enjoying a sunny afternoon with her two little ones at the playground. She bumped into an old school chum who had never seen her boys. The friend was taken with both children: Ryan, the animated and talkative two-year-old, with sandy blond hair and steel blue eyes, and Tommy, who at four months, was his usual, smiley self. She suggested that Adrienne take the boys to a place nearby where they're looking for kids to do a diaper commercial.

When the three of them arrived, the room filled with children and parents. Adrienne checked with the receptionist, and mentioned her referral. They were brought in immediately, ahead of all those who'd been waiting. As she was relaying all this on the phone to me, she exclaimed, "It really is who you know!"

True. At one time I was in a business that required meeting new people continually. One word that was on everyone's lips was "networking". If you knew one person, you could use that name to arrange a meeting with someone else.

Sooner or later we will end up at the famous Pearly Gates. Once there, no networking will be necessary. There will be no appointments and no waiting. We will be asked, in essence, "Who do you know?" And when the answer is "Jesus", we will be ushered right in.

It is definitely Who you know.

Major and Minor

The Lord made you; He formed you in the womb and he will help you. Isaiah 44:2

By late morning I had finally gotten myself outside. Armed with a pair of trusty clippers, I was ready to tackle the overgrown bushes in the back yard. I was getting into it and having fun chopping and trimming. All of a sudden I realized I was hot as a firecracker and about to have a heat stroke. I threw all the branches in a pile and jumped in the water to cool off.

That was when I noticed the bracelet my husband had given me was no longer on my wrist. I was angry with myself for wearing it to do yard work.

Carefully I moved the cuttings, one by one, watching for the bracelet to fall. All the while, I was looking at where Iid been working. It would be nearly impossible to spot it in the high grass or the flower bed rocks.

I said to God, "Lord, you know everything. So you know where EVERYTHING is. Therefore, you know where my bracelet is. It is not the biggest thing in the world, but it is sentimental to me. I should have taken it off, but I didn't. Now, Iim asking you to show me where it is, and – to please let it be in plain view."

I finished moving the whole trash pile, sighed, and looked up. There, on the decking, was the lost bracelet. It was perfectly curled on a narrow piece of wood between two cracks.

I thought, God is SO nice! He not only loves me, but He likes me! He shows me in the most real ways. Maybe He dispatched an angel to lay it there for me to find.

In the big picture, it's a pretty minor thing to lose a bracelet. It's major, though, when God so clearly reveals his caring in the ordinary things and our everyday lives. And if God takes care of minor things like this, how much more then will He take care of us, and the important, major issues in our lives?

Mercy!

"Shouldn't you have had mercy on your fellow servant just as I had on you?" Matthew 18:33

Once a week I meet for share-and-prayer. Last time we met, a regular in the group brought a visitor without checking first to see if it would be okay. That is my special place to share candidly. I felt intimidated with a new person present, and was reluctant to say much when it was my turn. The whole time I was thinking, "Forgive her for bringing her friend. Bless, not curse. I forgive her."

That evening, I was reading one of Corrie Ten Boom's books, in which she shared a story about forgiving someone who had wronged her in a letter. A friend told her to "forgive, and 'burn the black and white'." Symbolicly, I 'burned the black and white', and forgave my friend. Just then, these words came into my mind: "Mercy triumphs over rightousness." I thought, "What does that have to do with anything?" With my 'spiritual ears', I heard, "It's better to err on the side of mercy." It hit me. It's not about forgiveness. It's not about being right or wrong. It's about mercy.

I remembered a story where the ruling church criticized Jesus. They said, in essence, "What nerve you have! Picking grain and eating it on the Sabbath. That is clearly against the rules. What's the matter with you? You know better!" To which, Jesus replied, "We were hungry. Was man made for the sabbath, or sabbath for the man?"

I think I got it. My friend brought her guest along and looked at it as a kindness toward her. She had shown mercy. Mercy! Mercy triumphs over righteousness. Mercy triumphs over judgment. Thank God we have a merciful God. How I want to be like Him.

Mixing Up the Pronouns

At the name of Jesus every knee should bow, and every tongue confess that Jesus Christ is Lord.   Philippians 2:10-11

At two and a half years, Ryan is Mr. Independence. An adorable pint-sized blue eyed cutie, he is definitely feeling his 2 year old oats. Frequently his mom hears him say, "My do it myself!" When she is helping dress him, he might spout, "Him put him socks on him feet himself!" His own rendition of a song on TV, sung at the top of his little lungs, is "Bob the Builder, can him fix it? Yes! Him can!"

His PopPop and I have kiddingly adopted the speech pattern, because it reminds us of him, trying to be all grown up. We think it is just the cutest thing. All too soon he will quit mixing up the pronouns and get them in the right order.

Pronouns can be an indication of who's in charge. Or, who thinks he or she is in charge. Too often a rebellious spirit towards God invades my speech. I hear myself saying misplaced pronouns along these lines: "I can do it !" instead of, "He can do it". Or, "I want" rather than, "He wants".

In all twelve step programs, there are lots of pronouns, in the right order. A tiny paraphrase of the first three steps are: 1)I can't. 2)He can. 3)I think I'll let Him.

Today I will ask the Holy Spirit to adjust my thoughts and speech so that I do not mix up the important pronouns.

No Name Tags

"I will not forget you! See, I have engraved you on the palms of my hands." Isaiah 49:15-16

It was Saturday morning and I decided to try and beat the crowd to the grocery store. I was the checkout lane when I overheard a customer telling the cashier that she had just gotten back from a trip to her class reunion. She bubbled, explaining how much fun it was to see people from "'way back then". As she continued on about how much everyone had changed, she said, "In fact, it's a good thing we had name tags, or we might not have known each other!"

Time does have a way of doing that. Isn't it good to know that there's someone who will always know us, even without name tags, no matter how life or aging may have changed our appearances?

We are told, in Jeremiah 1:5, that our wonderful heavenly Father has known us since before "'way back when". He always recognizes us and He is filled with delight every time He looks at us.

That's good news!

No Walls

"At that moment the curtain of the temple was torn in two from top to bottom." Matthew 27:51

Each year, at holidays, seems like the same thing comes up time and again with one of our relatives. No matter how hard I try, sharing, honest intimacy, and vulnerability seem impossible.

This past holiday season it dawned on me that if my life was a circle, this person would be a dot on it. Perhaps there would be a thick concrete wall between me and the dot, but she was just one person. All the rest of the people in my life would be represented by the infinite number of dots that make up the entire remaining circumference of the circle. And there would be no walls between me and all of those dots.

This was a very cool revelation. So, there's a wall at one tiny intersection. Deal with it, "take the best and leave the rest".

I was thinking about this and found myself humming, "and the walls came tumbling down" , an old gospel song about when the walls came down at Jericho.

I thought about the great city of Berlin, Germany. Berlin had a wall dividing the east and west sectors of the city after the war. Not too many years ago, that wall was torn down. Now the city is a thriving place again, enjoying its unification.

When Christ was crucified, He died as a ransom for our lives; He was the living sacrifice. As He atoned for our sin(s), the wall came down between us and God.

No walls! Thank you, Lord.

Notes

Impress them on your children. Talk about them when you sit at home and when you walk along the road, when you lie down and when you get up. Tie them as symbols on your hands and bind them on your foreheads. Write them on the doorframes of your houses and on your gates.   Deuteronomy 6:7-9

Passing notes was dangerous. But it was fun. "Mary, Susan says that Johnnie likes Barbara. Do you like him? Check YES or NO." Or, "Can I see your homework?" Or, the not-so-smart, "Don't you just hate this class? It is so b-o-r-i-n-g!"

If you got caught writing, passing, or reading a note in class, the consequences could vary. At the least, you might suffer embarrassment, such as having the note read to the whole class. At worst, you could be sentenced to detention.

Last December, my husband and I were in NYC when they were experiencing bitter cold and record snows. We bundled up one afternoon and took the subway up toward Central Park. It is always a magnificent place. This particular day the snow made it purely magical.

God began to write and pass notes to me. "See the deep blue sky? I made it for you." "When the squirrel hops on the fence again, it means I'm sending you a hug." "That white blanket, covering the bridge there, is a present for you today!"

When God passes a note to us, no one gets into trouble. He just wants to get our attention so that we'll open them and read them.

God's notes: the best notes ever written, passed, or read.

Out of Control

"I am the true vine, and my Father is the gardener." John 15:1

My husband loves working in the yard. The rose bed on the side of the house is one of his projects. After several weeks of neglect, he went out this morning and found the bed in disarray.

The bushes were out of control. Some of the stems were taller than the windows. Leaves were chewed up from bugs and spotted with black mildew fungus. Worst of all, the buds were small, few, and malformed. That's not too good, since the whole purpose of the bushes is to enjoy the flowers.

He got busy cutting them way back. Then he sprayed for insects, fertilized, and mulched the bed. It looks great now. Soon we'll have beautiful, large roses to cut for the kitchen table. He will have to go back and tend to them again soon, however, if the bushes are to stay in good shape.

When left to my own devices, how quickly I get out of control. I go in all kinds of directions, lose my calm and get "buggy". The worst part is that the 'fruit', or what is produced, is small and unhealthy.

How wonderful that I have Someone to prune and discipline me so that large, beautiful roses will be the result. Now, all I have to do is let Him.

If you're interested, there is more information about:

Pen Pals

"I thank my God every time I remember you in all my prayers."
Philippians 1:3

A long time ago, in elementary school, I vaguely recall a class project where we all had pen pals in another country. Summer vacations and trips, too, provided opportunities for pen pals for my sister and me. The letters would fly back and forth for a few months with our new best friends.

A couple of years ago I received an email from Deborah B., a reply to an inspirational message posted on the Internet. Deborah wrote a lengthy, encouraging note. I was drawn to her, and to her spirit.

So I emailed her back. Thus began a special friendship with someone I know only through correspondence. Someday we will meet; meanwhile we write about our families, our work, and our faith. It never ceases to amaze me how she continually blesses me with her insightful comments and prayers. It is as though the Lord himself speaks through her at times.

There's another person I've not yet met who also blesses me in measureless ways. His name used to be Saul. After some interesting experiences, God changed it to Paul. He wrote these epistles that are in the Bible. Sometimes I think he wrote the letters just for me.

The Bible was written under the inspiration of the Holy Spirit. Now there is my forever pen pal. Thank you Lord!

Perspective

"Let us hold unswervingly to the hope we profess, for He who promised is faithful." Hebrews 10:23

Sorting through fifty years of stuff was an incredible journey back in time through our parents' earthly sojourn. My sister and I were sitting on the living room sofa, which still had the arm covers on it. Boxes of photos and letters and saved treasures were mounded up around us. We always joked about there being a lot to go through after Dad died, especially that attic!

We talked and cried, and it was evident how my sister sees and remembers things about our Dad one way, while I remember another. We were kids who grew up in the same family, yet viewed and related to our mom and dad in different ways.

Our dad was the same person always. Whether with my sister or with me, he was still "Daddy". Our different views of him did not change who he was at all. It was just our perspective.

That may be how God's kids, brothers and sisters in the church, view and relate to God. Individually. Perhaps the views and relationships to God are from very different perspectives.

Yet God is ALWAYS the same, unswerving and unchanging. Faithful. El Shaddai. El Elyon Adonai. The much loved hymn, *Great Is Thy Faithfulness*, says there is no shadow of turning with Him. He is the same yesterday, today, and forever.

Isn't it SO wonderful that in our lives, where everything is constantly changing, there is something/Someone who is not? It is a great comfort to me; a foundation on which to safely build and live.

Yes, that is good news.

Pools

"Come to me, all you who are weary and burdened, and I will give you rest."   Matthew 11:28

Last night it rained; lots of rain; lots of thunder and lightning. This morning the river seemed to be hustling along more rapidly than yesterday.

From our condo balcony, I spied a small pool and kept watching it for fish. The guide that accompanied us on our first fly-fishing adventure said to look for trout in the pools of the river. Sure enough, when the sun was full out, shining down, I could see a beautiful rainbow trout. He was so still I'd have thought he was dead if he hadn't been upright in the water.

In the quieter spots of our lives - the pools - where there's not a lot of motion, there is still something going on. There may not be the hustle-bustle, rush and turmoil of everyday life. Yet all around is a bubbling, effervescent world whose waters flow around us continually.

There is still life there, in the resting; life and renewal and refreshment. When it is time, we move out of the pool and into the current, back into the rapid flow of the river.

In the book of songs, in the Bible, it says, *"Be still, and know that I am God."* Thank God for the pools He provides for us in our lives.

R & R

He is my mighty rock, my refuge.   Psalm 62:7

I was getting ready to go away for a few days with my husband. In the heat of summer it is a treat for us to visit a cooler climate. I kept thinking, "R & R". Can't wait! Rest and Relaxation was what I had in mind. A few other combos or R &R would fit also: Renewal, Rejuvenation, Refreshing. Packing completed, I went to my desk to catch up on some Email. The little paperweight caught my eye. A small, rough rock, only about an inch and a half across; a gift from a friend many years ago. In big red letters, "SALLY", and under it: "Psalm 62:6, 7, 8". Turning it over, I read, "Giant Killer".

King David speaks those verses in the Bible so beautifully. God alone: David's rock, fortress, refuge where no enemy can reach him. He had his "Goliath", and we all have "giants" in our own lives.

My paraphrase of those verses in the book of Psalms is, R & R - Rock & Refuge. The Lord is my strong and steady rock, He is my refuge, my safe place.

I keep my little painted rock there, on my desk, to remind me I don't have to fight the things that come into my life that loom large, and I don't know how I can face them. Jesus, my Rock and Refuge, will take care of them, and me, too.

R & R - more than just rest and relaxation. Thank God!

Small Things

"... the truth, unless you change and become like little children, you will never enter the kingdom of heaven."   Matthew 18:3

Boarding the plane in Ft. Lauderdale, Florida, I noticed there were a lot of kids grouped ahead of me. Sixty-five, to be exact, were headed for summer camp. Once onboard, the airline attendant cruised the aisle, checking paperwork against who was actually seated in which seat. "It's too early for this," she quipped, with a twinkle in her eye, "but I know who the ringleaders are!"

The younger kids were so obviously excited as they chattered and laughed. During take-off, their arms went up in the air as if they were on a roller coaster. The older ones exchanged knowing glances that said, "Glad we are more mature than that."

Girls with very long, straight hair, sporting at least one toe ring on each sandaled foot, and boys in baggies and T-shirts moving back and forth in the aisle and climbed over seats with hand-held electronic devices. Adult passengers read newspapers, looked at cell phones that couldn't be turned on yet, and napped.

The little ones' exuberance sustained for the entire flight. Every single part of their experience was an adventure to be celebrated, from the video headsets to the drink cart and the telephones on the seat backs. No doubt, the kids were all looking forward to getting to the camp destination. However, it didn't diminish the full joy of the moment. Their excitement was in the present. Isn't it great to be a kid?

The best things in life do come in small packages. A little wooden placque in our home reads, "God's biggest blessings are little ones." Each new day, I will hopefully be aware of His gift of the precious present... in the small things.

Smooth Stones

One of the earliest Sunday school stories I recall hearing is the one about David and Goliath. David was a shepherd boy who came up against the gigantic warrior, Goliath, and with just a slingshot and a few little stones.

What a hero! He zapped the enemy in one fell blow, straight to the head. Here's the story, from the Bible (17th chapter of 1st Samuel): *"Then he took his (shepherd's) staff in his hand, chose five smooth stones from the stream, put them in the pouch of his shepherd's bag and, with his sling in his hand... David said to the Philistine(giant), 'You come against me with sword and spear and javelin, but I come against you in the name of the Lord Almighty, the God of the armies of Israel, whom you have defied. ... This day the Lord will hand you over to me, and I'll strike you down... All those gathered here will know that it is not by sword or spear that the Lord saves; for the battle is the Lord's, and he will give all of you into our hands.' ... Reaching into his bag and taking out a stone, he slung it and struck the Philistine on the forehead. So David triumphed ... without a sword in his hand he struck down the Philistine and killed him."*

The stones David selected were smooth; not big, heavy boulders. Small stones that had been continually washed by the river waters. They were more fit for use against the enemy than rougher, larger, more rugged stones.

David knew. He had spent a lot of time outdoors, by himself, taking care of the flocks of sheep for his father. He'd had plenty of time to practice with his slingshot. He knew how to use it.

In our journeys, as we are constantly washed by the waters of life, we too become more smooth; more fit to be used. As I was thinking of this, I couldn't help but think that it would be good for me to quit struggling so often, and to just go with the flow.

Smooth stones are good.

Special Sundays

"On the first day of the week... " Luke 24:1

Last Easter Sunday was such a special day. Sundays in general are special to people for a variety of reasons such as a day off, sleeping in, or how about food? (I thought of hot fudge sundaes; yummy!)

Maybe it means getting up early, rushing around, getting kids ready, going to church as usual - and looking all calm and happy when you get there.

When I was a child, Sundays meant afternoon outings with my dad such as baseball games or long walks to the park, or maybe ice cream. We didn't see much of him during the week; he went to work before I got up and came home after I went to bed. So Sundays were special.

With our kids, Sundays has been a family day. When they were little, we did simple things with them with mostly everyone sticking around the house. For years, now, we've had a hamburger cookout on Sunday at noon. Our kids and grandkids like getting together and it makes our Sundays special.

No matter how great our Sundays might be, the very best Sunday ever was the day we call Easter Sunday. That was the day Jesus came alive again, after having been dead. It was the day He first talked to people in his resurrected form.

Every day can be Easter Sunday for us as we encounter the risen Christ in our daily lives. That is truly good news!

Staying Connected

"I am the vine; you are the branches. If a man remains in me and I in him, he will bear much fruit; apart from me you can do nothing." John 15:5

It was a wonderful snowy day; just windy. You could hear that wind whistling through the trees. The thin, spindly tree that I could see outside the living room window was being seriously blown about. All the leaves were gone from the tree, save for a tiny reddish-brown one at the very top of the tree. It clung tenaciously as the wind whipped it.

The little leaf was enduring the hardship of a mountain winter. Spring would soon arrive and the tree would bud and fill with new leaves. It looked like the little leaf would make it. It would survive and enjoy the new spring and lazy summer before autumn and another winter would come.

Winter storms come into all of our lives. If you haven't experienced one, you surely will. Sometimes our personal winters cause us to abandon or turn our backs on whatever (or whomever) we're connected to.

When we suffer the pain of divorce, miscarriage, job loss, or any number of things that come our way in life's journey, there are times when we don't feel like hanging on. It simply seems too hard.

In the bible, in the book of John, Jesus tells us He is the vine (tree) and we are branches. If we stay connected to the tree, we can weather any storm. That's a hope we can hold onto and a promise we can claim. Staying connected will never get any better than that.

Stuck in Jerusalem

"... you will be my witnesses in Jerusalem, and in all Judea and Samaria, and to the ends of the earth." Acts 1:8

For most of my life I have heard the term "the great commission". That's what we're supposed to do as believers, which is to share the good news ("gospel") with other people. It's based on a verse in the bible where Jesus was in Jerusalem (after God raised Him from the dead). Jesus was addressing his disciples just before He left the earth and went back to heaven.

I was thinking about this recently. I don't travel to other countries. I don't really even want to go away and do missionary work. So I wondered, "Can I be a "witness" if I never get to third world countries?

We have a large, immediate and extended, family. Not a huge family, but nice sized, and all living close by. We span four generations. Most of the family gatherings take place at our home and a lot of the family networking is done through me. Somehow, this seems to occupy the bulk of my time and I love it. Nothing in the whole world makes me happier than my wonderful family.

Of all the many blessings God has given me, my family is the greatest. And this is my "Jerusalem". The verse says first in Jerusalem - then (concentrically) to other places.

I'm pretty much stuck in "Jerusalem", and glad of it. What better place to share good news?!

Surprise!

*"For I know the plans I have for you," declares the LORD ,
"plans to prosper you and not to harm you, plans to give you
hope and a future." Jeremiah 29:11*

Do you like surprises? Some do, some don't. My husband doesn't
like surprises very much. He likes a plan and knowing what
comes next. When he turned forty, I gave him a big surprise
party and that's how I found out.

Several years ago, I heard a message by Lloyd Ogilvie, who later
became chaplain of the United States Senate. It was about a
surprise party he had been given. At first, he was upset, because
he viewed it as one more interruption in his plans for that day.

Later, after he'd thought about it, he realized that's what life is: a
series of interruptions. It's kind of like God saying, "Surprise!"

We make plans, God laughs. Life goes on, with our schedules
being continually interrupted. All the while, Jehovah has
surprise, unexpected plans for us.

I'm not sure that I'm a control freak, but admittedly I like to be in
control a lot. We probably all like to be in control to some
degree, of ourselves, others, circumstances, and even the future.
It's an illusion, of course. Fortunately, we aren't in control, and
God is.

The next time things don't go quite the way I'd planned and
expected, hopefully I will hear God's voice saying, "Surprise!"

The Knot's Got a Name

"Call upon me in the day of trouble; I will deliver you, and you will honor me."   Psalm 50:15

Down in the Keys there is a bait and tackle shop named Captain Hook's. It's crammed full of... fishing 'stuff'. Small signs can be seen on the walls, such as, "I've only got one nerve left, and you're on it." For some reason that came to mind as I was dealing with issues regarding my aging father, particularly the car. Maybe you can relate to this: we didn't want him driving any longer. His eyesight is very bad and he has senile dementia. He was determined that he was going to keep driving. Only around town, of course, "Just to church, and the cemetery. Maybe the bank or grocery, but only in the daytime."

By the third time we had to go to another city to pick him up, my patience began to run out. We learned that he'd been driving around for several hours and had no idea where he was. I don't know who I was more worried about, him or the person he might hit. But I did know I was coming to the end of my rope.

Now, praying about all of this would have been wise. I'm sorry to say that I was trying to figure it out on my own. Often I'd picture the small poster of a kitten, hanging by its little paws on a clothesline, that was captioned, "Hang in there, baby."

A popular saying advises, "When you get to the end of your rope, tie a knot in it." It is best to go to the Lord first when we have problems. But when we don't, all else fails and we're at the end of our rope, it's good to remember that the knot has a name: Jesus.

We finally did pray, turning my dad and the whole situation over to the Lord. Not long afterward, he decided to give the car up to someone very much in need of transportation.

Jesus is the best 'knot' name. Hopefully, however, I can remember to go to Him in prayer before I get that far next time.

The Gold Bathing Suit

...over all these... put on love, which binds them all together in perfect unity.   Colossians 3:14

Last night three of our young grandchildren had a sleepover. Watching them swim before bedtime, my mind traveled back to when my sister and I were kids. For ten weeks each summer we were in absolute heaven, at a small lakeside cabin, where our parents had spent their honeymoon.

The year I was eight, I had a gold lame bathing suit. I felt like the queen, or at the very least, Esther Williams. What I couldn't do in that suit! Synchronized ballet swimming had nothing on my moves. Or so I thought. Once I donned the gold bathing suit, I was invincible in the water.

Sometimes I catch myself dressing a certain way according to my mood. If I am feeling confident, maybe a classy, together looking outfit, complete with jewelry. If I feel blue or down in the dumps, a sloppy T-shirt,cut-offs, and a ponytail might do it.

In the Bible, book of Isaiah, it says, to put on a garment of praise for the spirit of heaviness. Singing along to some praise and worship music definitely brightens up my depression.

So here's the question: what are you wearing today? No matter what it is, God's love and light fit perfectly over it. They're the one-size fits all that really does, any and every day.

The Whisper Test

"You are precious and honored in my sight, and because I love you... " Isaiah 43:4

A young girl with a cleft palate and speech challenges was fortunate to be in a classroom setting with a wise teacher. Each week the children would take the "whisper test". One at a time, the teacher called them forward. She would whisper in their ear a question, like "What did you have for breakfast this morning?", or "What is your Mom's first name?" Then, when the child answered correctly, she'd exclaim, "Right! You pass!"

One week was a bit different. This time when the teacher called the little girl up, she whispered into her ear, "I wish you were my little girl." That was a magical moment for the child. It was the turning point from her embarrassment and her insecurities. To know she was loved and valued changed her life.

Ever wonder if anyone really loves and values you? I have a pretty normal life, with a lot of love in it. Still, there have been moments when I have asked that question. How wonderful that we all have a Father who loves and values us unconditionally, with our warts and all. That's a tough one to comprehend.

Sometimes when I pray, just chatting and talking things over with my Father, I'm sure that I hear Him whisper, "I'm so glad you are my little girl!"

Try praying and talking with Him. Most assuredly you will receive a special whisper, and loving message from our Father.

That is good news.

The Philippians Four-Six Basket

"Do not fret or have any anxiety about anything, but in every circumstance and in everything, by prayer and petition (definite requests), with thanksgiving, continue to make your wants known to God." Philippians 4:6 AMP

Can you still smell the vinegar we added to the dye tablets every year to color Easter eggs? The trickiest part of all was to put a pin prick in the ends of the egg and blow it out, then dip it. I never could do that .

It is 'the season'. At stores all over our city, there are ready made, pre-assembled Easter baskets of all sizes and kinds on display. They are beautifully arranged and wrapped with everything in them from chocolate-covered-marshmallow-peanut-butter eggs to small, soft cuddly bunnies to tiny digitalized computer games.

Although it's spring and the weather's gorgeous, nonetheless I found myself in a blue funk not long ago. There was major crisis, nothing was seriously wrong; I was just out of sorts. I thought that perhaps I had taken on a few too many projects. I seemed to be feeling overwhelmed by those nebulous things that float around in the background.

Something or someone, triggered my memory, and The Basket came to mind. It has always worked, so, immediately I envisioned it. As always, it was at the foot of the cross. Just sitting there, empty. (Funny, it is always empty.) As quickly as persons, projects, situations, or upcoming events came to mind, I put them into The Basket. Whatever came to mind; in it went.

Soon the thoughts slowed down, then there was nothing more to put in. "At least not for now," I thought. I actually felt lighter, physically. "Amazing!" I said out loud to myself, even though I figured that is what would happen. My attitude turned right around.

Last evening I read a magazine article which prompted me to give my basket a new name. The article was about anxiety, and it said we can feel overwhelmed and tired because we are carrying around burdens we don't need to shoulder. It was based on a bible verse I have known for years. The first half is: don't worry, don't fret, don't be anxious. The second half is: tell God your definite requests and be thankful for everything He has done for you.

From now on, I'll be putting my "stuff" into the Philippians Four-Six Basket. Then I can get on with the second half of the verse!

The Rolling Store

If you....know how to give good gifts to your children, how much more will your Father in heaven give the Holy Spirit to those who ask him!   Luke 11:13

Once a week the rattly old bus would wind its way up the mountainside to the few cabins and cottages on Lake Delaware. Each week, my sister and I were waiting and had our allowance ready.

It was always exciting to climb the steps and look into "The Rolling Store". It had been renovated and outfitted with lots of intriguing shelves filled with groceries and other items. While Mom bought a few things, we had time to peruse the candy shelves, and choose from the many mouthwatering penny items. Mary Janes, Necco wafers, Good 'n Plenty, etc. A small sack to last the week and we were happy campers.

Have you heard the saying, "All good things come to those who wait"? The store came to us, we didn't have to go looking for things to buy that we wanted. Likewise, God will bring to us what we need. Doors and windows will open.

Today is unfolding just as planned. What I need will come to me today, without my searching everywhere for it. All I need to do is trust in the Lord, and in His plan for me. Thank you, my wonderful Father.

Section III

*Jesus Christ the Messiah is always
the same, yesterday, today,
yes and forever*   **Hebrews 13:8**

*Now we see but a poor reflection as in a mirror; then we shall
see face to face. 1 Corinthians 13:12*

20/20 Vision

There it was, all shiny and new, attached to the wall by the
bathroom counter. My husband had kindly put up the oversize
magnifying mirror I'd bought. There it was, all shiny and new,
attached to the wall by the bathroom counter. Now I could
actually see to apply my make-up. Wonderful!

My eyesight has never been very good. At seven years old I
started wearing glasses. Not too many kids that age wear glasses,
and I got teased about them. After I turned forty, well, suffice it
to say my vision didn't improve any. I sought laser surgery so I
wouldn't have to wear tri-focal lenses, but wasn't a candidate.

Then one day I discovered a local shop selling magnifying
mirrors. What a great invention. It doesn't make my vision
20/20, even with glasses. But it's way better than it was.

In Genesis it says They made man in Their image and it was
VERY good. Not just "good". When God looks at us He sees
us as we are, with 20/20 vision. At the same time He sees us as
we will be, with 100/100 vision. That's perfect. And very good
news.

"I have told you these things, so that in me you may have peace."   John 16:33

A Lot of Questions

If I live to be a hundred there are some things I will never understand. Why do some people live, and some die? Why do some people have debilitating diseases and others, perfect health? Why do some have loads of money and others struggle to survive? Why do some get caught and others go free? Why do some people recover and get well, others don't?

Don't we all wonder about these questions? I do, from time to time, and my answer is always the same, "I don't know." I don't know much, and even less the older I get. My list of questions I want to ask when I get to heaven is pretty long.

In this life, there are a lot of mysteries. We will not humanly understand many things.

Yet underlying all the unknowns is the one great thing we do know: God is still on his throne. He is still sovereign, still in charge. He knows what is going on. He doesn't just wake up one morning, look down, and say, "Oh my gosh! Look at that!!"

We may not be able to trust in the system, in people, in circumstances or luck.

But we can trust in the Lord God. And the promise is that one day, every tear shall be wiped away. Every sickness, every injustice, every heartache.

Jesus said we will surely have troubles here on earth, but to be undaunted and confident because He has overcome the world's power to harm us permanently.

Bottom-line, the answer to all these questions really is- hang onto the promise, and hold onto the Lord.

When I begin, I will also make an end.   1 Samuel 3:12

A New Beginning

A friend, Lynn, was sharing how one morning, while trying to make coffee, the light in the coffee pot switch kept blinking unsteadily. She plugged it into a new outlet, and it exploded. Lights flashed and the old switch burned out. "It's a new year", she said, "and maybe I need a new plug to burn out any flimsy switch in my
life! "

I'm not too big on new year's resolutions, nor do I think God is interested in our calendar which says it's a new year. To Him it might be just another 'day'.   I do think that He is interested in our repentance and surrender in a new way. Maybe it's time for me to take an inventory, and do just that. Again.

Every ending is a new beginning. God has a plan for us in 2004, as well as for the rest of our lives. A lot of new beginnings, and they're good. One of my favorite bible verses is Jeremiah 29:11, "For I know the plans I have for you," declares the Lord , "plans to prosper you and not to harm you, plans to give you hope and a future." It's a great promise.

Today I'm thankful for today, a new beginning.

"I tell you the truth, anyone who will not receive the kingdom of God like a little child will never enter it." Mark 10:15

A Plus

McCallen has great big-as-saucer round brown eyes. Her hair is shiny and dark. She has a dynamite smile and creamy olive complexion. And she's our very wonderful, special grandchild. McCallen is as beautiful on the inside as she is on the outside, with her gentle, loving, kind nature.

A couple of years ago, her parents were with her at a new school for some testing. The facilitator had been showing McCallen oversized flash cards, with symbols and pictures on them, and asking her to talk about them.

After a while, she began to fidget. She'd about had enough when the next card came up with a plus sign on it. Without hesitation, her eyes lit up and she responded enthusiastically. "Jesus!".

Sometimes kids catch on quicker than "grown-ups".
During the years of Jesus' teaching and ministry here on earth, He once said, *"I praise you, Father, Lord of heaven and earth, because you have hidden these things from the wise and learned, and revealed them to little children."* (Matthew 11:25)

A "plus" usually means extra or a bonus, or the buzz word, "perk". To McCallen, the plus sign represented a cross. I believe she knows a cross is not just a plus, but everything, because it means Jesus.

....how many times shall I forgive my brother when he sins against me? Matthew 18:21

Another Name

My sister was named for our aunt. She never really liked her name. When she began writing , she changed the spelling of her name from the male version to the female, but ended up going back to the original. Performers usually take a stage name. Many authors have a pseudonym. Some people add a name, like at confirmation.

God has many names which describe facets of His character. Jehovah Rapha (The Lord who heals) and Jehovah Jireh, (The Lord our provider) are a couple. He has another name I have given Him. Jehovah the God of Another Chance.

The other day on the phone I got my feelings hurt by a candid comment. He apologized, wanted another chance to rephrase what he'd said. I was quickly weighing the pros and cons, while that little voice inside was saying, "YES, give him another chance."

How many times in just one day do I want somebody else to allow me another chance?

For something I have done - or not done.

Mahatma Ghandi is quoted as saying, "If we practice an eye for an eye and a tooth for a tooth, soon the whole world will be blind and toothless."

In the Bible there is an account of Peter asking Jesus just how many times he should forgive someone. Peter thought he was being so magnanimous by offering to do that not once, not twice, but seven times. Seven is a number symbolic of perfect, complete, or whole, so Peter felt sure he was being more than generous. Jesus gently corrected his thinking when He said not seven times, but seventy times seven. In other words, no number large enough to express how many times.

The Lord is always willing to forgive us when we mess up and make mistakes. There is no set time when He says, "That's it! No more chances for you!" Yes, He has many names, including The God of ALWAYS Another Chance.

You have made known to me the path of life; you will fill me
with joy in your presence. Psalm 16:11

Anytime, Anywhere

For nearly a year we had been planning our big family vacation.
My husband and I, our children and spouses and the 5 oldest
grandkids were going out west to a ski resort on Spring Break
week. It was a very big deal, especially since we all live in a
warm climate. First morning 'most everyone headed to the ski
slopes. My daughter, a new mom, went for some R&R at a spa,
and I set out for an early walk.

Light snow was flurrying, and even against a grey sky it was
beautiful. Not too far away was a church. I eased into a small
back pew. Communion was being celebrated during the service.
As I made my way up front, I looked out across the people.

So many different faces, so many different reasons that might
have brought them there. No doubt many had come to simply
worship our Lord. Others, though, perhaps out of desperation,
or with a faint hope. I thought, so many different cries of the
heart, yet God hears them all.

Many times over the years I had sought out this peaceful place.
It had always been a safe, sheltering place to pray.

It is wonderful to have the opportunity to go to a church or place
of worship to seek God and meet with Him.

However, we can do that anytime, anywhere. No matter what is
on our minds, and what our needs or desires are, Jesus is always
available to us. Anytime, anywhere.

....you shall celebrate it as a festival to the Lord...   *Exodus 12:14*

As Long As Possible

Do you like birthdays? I love my birthday. So much so that I don't even mind what the double digits are registering. Holidays are for everyone. But your birthday is YOUR day.!

There is only one of you. That is something to celebrate! And I like to do it as long as possible. If I can stretch it out for a few days, that is good. The whole month is even better. My friends know how much I love my birthday, so each year they start booking dates, to get together and celebrate it, weeks before it gets here.

Actually I have 2 birthdays. First, the day my mother gave birth to me physically. Second, the day I was born spiritually. A conversation Nicodemus had with Jesus when he sneaked over in the cloak of darkness, went like this: Jesus declared, *"I tell you the truth, no one can see the kingdom of God unless he is born again. "How can a man be born when he is old?" Nicodemus asked. "Surely he cannot enter a second time into his mother's womb to be born.*

Jesus answered, "I tell you the truth, no one can enter the kingdom of God unless he is born of water and the Spirit. Flesh gives birth to flesh, but the Spirit gives birth to spirit. You should not be surprised at my saying, 'You must be born again.' The wind blows wherever it pleases. You hear its sound, but you cannot tell where it comes from or where it is going. So it is with everyone born of the Spirit." (John 3:3-8)

Here's the good news: every one of us can have 2 birthdays. If we believe in our hearts, and confess with our mouths, that Jesus is Lord, we will be born again, born a second time. We can celebrate every single day of the year.

And how about this: we can celebrate as long as we live, then even longer.! As long as possible, with God - eternity and forever.

.....though he stumble, he will not fall, for the Lord upholds him with his hand.   Psalm 37:24

Bam!

It was still early morning. Not much stirring. Even the neighborhood cat that lurks around the bird feeder hadn't shown up yet. The activities of a frisky baby squirrel caught my eye. "He is the youngest squirrel I've ever seen out there!" I thought.

He was so cute. Tiny face. Tail still thin and unfluffy. Running all over the wood roofing as if the chase was on. He began turning and hopping like a little bunny, darting back and forth. Clearly he was having the most wonderful playtime. Looked like his mom could have cared less what he was up to. She was ensconced at the cardinal feeder, merrily munching away.

He came up to the corner closest at the window where I was watching. All of a sudden, bam! He hit the ground with an awful sound. "Oh, man!" I whispered. At least it was the wood decking and not the concrete.

He was stunned, didn't move. Slowly he turned and sat up. He lifted his very tiny left paw. As it dangled, he cautiously licked it. After a minute he went over to the post and gingerly made his way up.

Once again, safe on the top beam, he began slowly to nurse his foot back to health. The mother squirrel never once checked on him or even glanced his way. The correlation crossed my mind. If we're on cruise control, let's say just going along, ordinary everyday, and inadvertently have an accident, we wouldn't be left to fend for ourselves the best we could. Fortunately, we have a "parent" who would immediately - if not before - check on us. He would be taking situation in hand to restore and heal us.

That's the kind of dad our heavenly Father is. Oh thank God!

We do not have a high priest who is unable to sympathize with our weaknesses, but...we have one (Jesus, the Son of God) who has been tempted in every way, just as we are-- Hebrews 4:15

Been There, Done That

This afternoon I was waving my arm back and forth underwater, hoping the weightlessness and buoyancy of the pool would help heal the tendonitis. In the past, my husband has suffered with arthritic problems in his shoulders and elbows. He would wince when turning a certain way, even in his sleep. I believed him, that it really hurt. I couldn't understand it though.

I can no longer say that, thanks to the trimming of the banana tree. The dead leaves kept getting droopier, so one morning I got out the long-handled clippers. Intrepidly, I tackled my project. Somehow I forgot about banana leaves being made of incredibly strong, fibrous material not unlike nylon. I had a good grip, twisted my forearm, and pop! I could feel the burning sensation.

It is true, you can't understand a person until you've walked in his shoes.

Nor can you, I think, truly trust him unless he's 'been there, done that'. In the Bible, it says Jesus understands everything about us. Everything. If that is so, then he has experienced all that we have.

As I pondered this, the thought crossed my mind, " I don't think so. He lived a long time ago and there's no way he's gone through what I have."

Then different stories from the bible came to mind. I thought how Jesus was shunned and rejected by not only strangers, but also by people he knew well. He was misunderstood continually, and misrepresented. He felt sadness, sorrow, and he grieved. He hurt and he got angry. He loved his mom, family, parties, his buddies. He was, at times, tempted to do wrong, perhaps even confused and unsure. And often he talked things over with his Father.

If each time there's a twinge of pain, my memory is jogged to recall that we have a Saviour who's "been there, done that" and I can trust Him, it will have been more than worth it.

Do not be anxious about anything, but in everything, by prayer and petition, with thanksgiving, present your requests to God. Philippians 4:6

Closed Up and Shut Down

Big, full anemone type flowers in bright, lemon yellows and neon pinks cluster about our front walkway. They really catch the eye, and they thrive in the brutal heat of our tropical days.

At night, however, they close up and shut down. The droopy gray-green succulent leaves look nearly dead. In fact you probably wouldn't even notice them at all.

Have you heard the saying, "Pray at night and give your problems to the Lord; He'll be up all night anyway."

It is so comforting to know that God is never closed up and shut down. (*Psalm 121:3...."He who watches over you will not slumber"*).

That is good news.

......and they were holding golden bowls full of incense, which are the prayers of the saints.   Revelation 5:8

DELETED

Hurriedly, I was trying to retrieve Email I had deleted by mistake. No such luck. It was gone from that big E- mailbox in the sky. I was reminded of old science fiction movies where a martian, or other outer-space individual, would get zapped. One beam of light and he was deleted. Gone.

This week my husband was sharing how much his spiritual heritage means to him. "Just think," he said, "of all the prayers that have been said for me by my parents, grandparents, and others. Who knows where I'd be if it weren't for all those prayers!"

Later, I thought about what Ben had said. None of the prayers offered in his name has ever been deleted. No prayer he has prayed has been erased, either. Nor mine. Nor yours.

It says in the final book of the Bible that all our prayers are stored in huge golden bowls in God's throne room.

All.

What an honor privilege, and blessing to pray. Each and every prayer is heard by God himself. And not one of them will ever be deleted. Not even by accident.

Be....alert. Your enemy the devil prowls around like a roaring lion looking for someone to devour. 1 Peter 5:8

Does it Feel Like a War?

The stony silence continued for days. On the surface, it looked like everything was fine. Life went on as usual. He went to work, I took care of the house, cooked, carpooled the kids everywhere. Everything was not fine, however. The disagreement my husband and I had hung in the air. It didn't feel like a battle, but I wasn't at peace. There was no resolve to it yet.

For months our country has been bombarded with facts and statements from the government telling us we are at war. Yet day to day, I don't feel like we're at war. There is no shortage of gasoline, or water, or food. No rationing. No massive drafting of young people to go overseas and fight.

Granted this is a different kind of war than ever before. In the light of some some recent info from the media, I realized that regardless of what it feels like, the reality is we are very much so in a war.

Yes, ever since 9-11 we have been in a full fledged war with terrorism. The face of the enemy looks like Islamic extremists, living all over the world, who will stop at nothing until they have taken over everywhere. All in the name of Allah, their 'god', who is not Jehovah God, the Lord of hosts.

We are all in another war every single day of our lives for as long as we live. This enemy is subversive, sneaky, and relentless also, and has a terrible plan for our lives. He doesn't want to simply distract, or deter us, from Godly living. He wants to ruin, wreck, and utterly destroy us.

Quite some time ago I heard a pastor make a thought-provoking remark, "If you don't know you're in a war, you've already lost the battle." So- even though we may not overtly feel we are in a moment-by-moment war with satan, we most assuredly are.

The good news is we know Who wrote the last chapter, and Who wins.

Look to the Lord and his strength; seek his face always.
Psalm 105:4

Expecting the Unexpected

Things didn't go quite like I'd planned today. "Imagine that," I thought. Well, if there is one thing in life we can be certain of, it's change. When our kids were growing up, I recall feeling strongly about preparing them for change in their lives, to understand the need to be flexible without compromising our values and who we are.

The names for the Lord God Almighty, our triune God, are many in the Old Testament scriptures. Among them are Jehovah Shammah, the God who is there. That is one of my favorites. Also Jehovah Nissi, the Lord our banner, who goes before us, and Jehovah Rohe, the God who heals.

My personal extra name for God is Jehovah Surprise, the God of the Unexpected. Not that anything happening catches Him off-guard. He's not up in heaven, looking down, exclaiming, "Oh my gosh! Look at that!" Rather, I'm the one who is continually surprised by events and people. Sometimes I even surprise myself. That is not always so great.

There's a saying, "We make plans and God laughs." And yet another saying, "Life is what happens while we're making other plans."

God may be full of surprises, yet He is still in control, still the sovereign God of the universe, still on His throne, the same yesterday, today, and forever.

The Lord's love and faithfulness is about the only thing we can expect in the midst of the unexpected. The good news is we *can* count on Him in our constantly ever-changing world.

See, I set before you today life and prosperity, death and destruction... life and death, blessings and curses. Now choose life, so that you and your children may live.
Deuteronomy 30:15-19

Imperceptibly Turning

Clearing out clutter, and sprucing up after the holidays, called for something new from the nearby garden shop. I picked a hardy houseplant and placed the pot outside where you could see it from the kitchen. It looked perfect out there.

One day I looked out the window and the plant was all bent over and facing the other way. It had gotten plenty of water, what happened? It looked so pretty before.

Seemed like that plant changed direction overnight. Of course, it didn't happen that fast. It was like time lapse photography. Each day, the little leaves turned their faces towards the sun. Imperceptibly, the plant was turning. Ever so slowly. And over a period of time, the difference was very noticeable.

Plants don't have a choice. They just do what they do. We, however, have a choice. We can choose what we look at, what we think about, what we absorb.

In our day-to-day lives, all the seemingly insignificant decisions we make, matter. As we turn in the direction of our focus, little by little, the choices pile up to create a definite, noticeable change.

The writer of Philippians, Paul, says: "Finally, brothers, whatever is true, whatever is noble, whatever is right, whatever is pure, whatever is lovely, whatever is admirable--if anything is excellent or praiseworthy--think about such things."

How beautiful we are when we make choices like this......no matter where we are planted!

God is our refuge and strength, an ever-present help in trouble.
Psalm 46:1

In the Night

Lucy is one of my husband's favorite relatives. She is a gentle person. Exactly the kind of mother, grandmother, aunt, or neighbor you would want. Her hair is white and curled, and patted down to cover the balding thinness. She walks bent over from the great hump on her back from osteoporosis.

Lucy always has a ready and listening ear. She always has something kind and encouraging to say. You just feel better being around her.

She stays busy with friends and family, but lives alone. Her husband and best friend of 45 years, died. I asked her, "How are you really doing?" She paused, then said, "It's hardest in the night. Everything is worse at night."

Lucy's peaceful and pleasant demeanor covers her real feelings of ongoing loneliness and anxiety. In the book of Samuel, in the Bible, it says we look at what we can see, but God looks at the heart.

Sometimes we look all "together" when really we are in our "night." God alone sees into our deepest heart of hearts. He knows what is written there.

He is always about the business of comforting us. He actually provides us with His very presence. That word of hope is real good news. Especially in the night.

.....they will all know me, from the least of them to the greatest.
Hebrews 8:11

It's Who You Know

Yesterday my daughter was enjoying a sunny afternoon, with
her two little ones, at the playground. She bumped into an old
school chum who had never seen her boys. The friend was taken
with both - Ryan, the animated and talkative 2 year old, with
sandy blond hair and steel blue eyes, and Tommy, who at 4
months was his usual smiley self. She suggested that Adrienne
take them to a place nearby where they're looking for kids to do
a diaper commercial.

When the three of them arrived, the room filled with children
and parents. Adrienne checked with the receptionist, and
mentioned her referral. They were brought in immediately,
ahead of all those who'd been waiting. As she was relaying all
this on the phone to me, she exclaimed, "It really is who you
know!"

True. At one time I was in a business that required meeting new
people continually. One word that was on everyone's lips was
"networking". If you knew one person, you could use that name
to finagle meeting someone else.

Sooner or later we will end up at the famous Pearly Gates. Once
there, no networking will be necessary. No appointments, no
waiting. We will be asked, in essence, "Who do you know?"
And when the answer is "Jesus", we will be ushered right in.

Definitely it is Who you know.

Now choose life...   *Deuteronomy 30:19, 1 Kings 18:32*

Life in the River

Enjoying a cup of coffee in the early morning quiet at our
vacation condo, I was watching the activity of the river below.
Due to a long drought, the water was way down. Rocks and
boulders I'd never seen before were in full view. A small white
piece of paper, or plastic, caught my eye. It was going 'round
and 'round in a tiny area almost entirely closed off by small
boulders. The whole time I watched, it never left the spot, just
continued to spin around.

That night it rained cats and dogs. Next morning, the river was
noticeably higher. It sang a bit louder and ran a little faster. The
white paper was no longer swirling in a circle. It was, instead,
wedged up against a rock close to the river's edge. It was safely
hugging the rock, just out of reach of the moving water. It
seemed the paper had no choice. It was stuck.

Sometimes I feel stuck in the river of life. Unlike the paper,
however, I have a choice. A long time ago God made a choice
that would bring people back to Him.

Through Jesus we have a choice: accept His life sacrifice for us,
get out of our own little whirlpool worlds and move downstream
with Him, or stay stuck in our self centered world while we cling
to some safe rock in the river.

I hope that daily I can remember to make the better choice, and
keep moving with the current. Even if momentarily, or
temporarily, I get caught in a holding pattern, I can choose to
move out and onward with Him.

Be still, and know that I am God.   Psalm 46:10

Listen to the Quiet

When the electricity went out recently, I was impressed with how quiet it was. We live with continual background noise. Indoors we have the sounds of air conditioning units, washers and dryers, TVs, computers, telephones, computers, fax machines, answer machines, stereos, and kids. Outdoors are lawnmowers, leaf blowers, trains, airplanes, insects, birds, animals, cars and cell phones.

We have all kinds of noise inside our heads, too. Past tapes, what others have said and done, things we have done or told ourselves. And what about the noise our hearts make? They laugh, cry, remember, and talk to us too!

I don't think of myself as somebody who leads a fast-paced, jet-set life. That is until I notice how long it takes me to relax and unwind.   Getting quiet doesn't happen quickly for me. Sometimes I even have to consciously work at it. Even David, songwriter extraordinaire, wise warrior, and anointed King of Israel, needed to be reminded by God to "Be still, and know that I am God." (Psalm 46:10)

It's a noisy world. And we all need a quiet place in the midst of all the noise. A safe place, where we can BE STILL, and hear the Lord.

He very much wants to tell us how much he loves us, and how unique and special we are to him.

Ask him to help you find a safe place, a place where you can go and listen to the quiet. Thank God he provides places for us, whether inside our mind and heart, or in a physical spot. Journey there and see what wonderful surprises Jesus has planned to share with you in this brand new day of Today that you've never seen before.

God is our refuge and strength, an ever- present help in trouble.
Psalm 46:1

Nearly Deadly

She was from another country. She tried hard to communicate
and fit in. She read books to learn the language. She watched TV
to study the vernacular.

She was a cheerful, pleasant, person. She hired out to different
families as a newborn nurse, taking care of babies. Long hours,
long nights, long weeks away from her new husband. And far,
far away from her home, family, friends, or anything familiar.
She had put all her trust and all her saving hope in the fellow
who married her and brought her to this country. She leaned on
him hard, looked to him for her every need.

Things seemed as if they were going pretty well. Then last week
they found her. She nearly died from an attempted suicide.

Drugs and alcohol were listed as the cause. But what really
nearly killed her was disillusionment. Her trust and hope had
been crushed beyond anything she could cope with. She had
made her husband the 'everything' in her life. When he took up
with a younger woman, her great giant hope crumbled.

People are just people; not perfect and not God. Sooner or later
people will say or do something that doesn't meet our
expectations and we will be disappointed. There is only One
Hope that will never, ever fail us. We can count Him.

Putting all our eggs in one basket will work only when the
basket is the Lord. There will never be a problem with Him not
meeting our standards or disappointing us. Jesus is, and will
always be, there to trust and lean on.

It's a promise! And it's for all of us who will believe in Him.
That's good news.

And I will do whatever you ask in my name, so that the Son may bring glory to the Father.   John 14:13

Networking and Name Dropping

Networking and name dropping were buzz words in the nineties. When I began attending workshops for songwriters, I learned early on how to network. As soon as I met with one person, I could use his/her name to get a meeting lined up with the next person. When I was writing, I had a friend who was well known as an author. Using her name at a conference opened all kinds of doors for me to talk to high powered people at the corporation.

We have each probably encountered someone who is a proverbial name dropper. He happens to mention the account he landed, and the persons or companies connected to it. She can't resist telling you the brand name sweater she's wearing; maybe initials are boldly advertised on her purse. At one time or another I have been guilty of all the above.

There is a name we can drop into our conversations with God anytime. He's not impressed, but talk about getting you everywhere. Jesus said to ask for anything in prayer, using His name. In turn, Jesus mentions our names to the Father..........

This kind of networking and name dropping is not only OK, it has been designed by God for our benefit, and His glory. The power in the name of Jesus is awesome. It is the name above all names.

With the Lord a day is like a thousand years, and a thousand years are like a day.   2 Peter 3:8

No Concept of Time

She was definitely a member of our family... Bailey, a beautiful twelve-year-old buff cocker spaniel. Over the years, we had had a lot of fun with Bailey. When she was a puppy, we'd go in and out of the house and watch how excited she would get every time we came back in. Each time she would go bonkers because she was so glad to see us. Her tail would just about wag off.

Bailey had no concept of time. If we were gone for hours, days, or just moments, she didn't know the difference. All she knew was we were gone, then we were there.

Our seven young grandchildren have no concept of time yet. They are always so happy to see us. Doesn't matter how much time has elapsed between seeing them last, they are always just so glad to see us when they do.

Adults do have a concept of time. And yet, time is a weird thing. The older we get, the more we wonder where it has gone.

God has an even different concept of time. Yet, each time He gazes on us, He is thrilled beyond measure. We are His creations, the works of His hands, and He loves us beyond anything we can comprehend.

We sometimes mess up and we're far from perfect, but He is just crazy about us - just the way we are!

That is good news.

And everyone who calls on the name of the LORD will be saved.
Joel 2:32, Acts 2:21, Romans 10:13

No Time

As a child, I was only concerned with what was going on "right now", living fully in the moment with no cares about anything else. Certainly I never gave a thought to dying. Even though we all die, sooner or later.

For the victims of the recent dreadful terrorist disasters, it was sooner, and not later. For them, there was no time. No time to take care of unfinished business. No time to say or do something they had planned to do someday (the 'Isle of Later'). No time to think about the hereafter - where they would be going, forever.

It is so easy to procrastinate and put things off, especially important decisions. I have the best intentions, yet getting "a round tuit" often gets left in the dust for immediate priorities.

But the most important decision we could ever make is one we don't have to put off, not for a single second. It's not something we can get somebody else to do for us, nor is it a lengthy, time-consuming task. It is simple:

Several places in the Bible (*) it says that if we seek the Lord honestly, with our hearts, and call on Him, we will be found by Him, and saved. Not just a few, not the called and chosen, but everyone. It also says that if we forsake him, He will reject us forever.

Today, while we have time, let 's be sure we have taken that step to seek the Lord, call on His name, and be found by Him. He is just waiting for that, with open arms and a loving heart.

(*) Isaiah 55:6, Proverbs 8:18, Deuteronomy 4:28-30, 1 Chronicles 28:10, Jeremiah 29:13, Amos 5:4

Therefore, if anyone is in Christ, he is a new creation; the old has gone, the new has come!   *2 Corinthians 5:17*

Rags at the Banquet

Once upon a time a man lived in the streets, clad only in the dirtiest and worst of rags. One day a person from the Palace saw him, and
approached him. There was going to be a banquet at the Palace, and he had instructions to come and invite people from the highways and byways. Would he like to come?

The man was indeed interested. However, he could not attend a banquet dressed in his rags. The Palace representative assured him they would exchange his rags for some suitable finery to wear to the banquet.

All was in order. The two arrived at the Palace where they went directly to the dressing chambers of the King. Servants took the filthy rags, bundled them in a little package, and proceeded to rub, scrub, and clean the man from top to bottom.

He was then allowed to choose his robes from the closets of the King. He was told that whatever he picked he would be able to keep, so he carefully examined all the many garments in the closet. He chose an exquisite inner garment of purest silk, and an outer robe of finest purple satin. He was ready for the banquet!

As they left the dressing quarters, the man grabbed his old rags. The servants told him to just leave them, because he wouldn't need them anymore. However, he insisted on taking the bundle with him. Even though he didn't need the rags now, he felt more secure somehow if he could just hold on to them.

In the Palace banquet hall, the festivities were about to begin. Nearly everyone was there, including the King himself. The man was seated, looking resplendent in his new attire. He hid his bundle of rags on his lap, underneath the tablecloth, so no one would see them.

The banquet was not to be believed! There was music and dancing, and every kind of delicacy imaginable. As the trays were passed, the beggar had difficulty getting the food onto his plate. He was constantly juggling the package of old rags on his lap, balancing it so it wouldn't fall off. It constantly distracted him from what was going on in the grand hall.

Eventually the evening ended and the great gala event was over. Everyone was stuffed to the gills except for the man clinging to his rag bundle. He was as hungry as when he had come in. He never had eaten even one morsel of the food. He had been too busy fixing and holding on to his old rags.

Today, Jesus invites all of us to God's great banquet, to leave our old ways and old rags, and to say, "Yes!" to Him and to a new and glorious way of living.

That is good news!

Then God said, "Let us make man in our image, in our likeness."
Genesis 1:26

Real or Reflected

The kids were jumping up and down, trying to get every adult in the place to look out the window at their new discovery. Wow! A field full of 'diamonds'?! The reason for all those 'gems', a reflection of the sun as it shone on the ice crystals in the snow. The sparkle and glitter was definitely dazzling.

As my husband and I were walking home later that evening, I was amazed at the number of stars we could see. With few streetlights, the stars, planets, even the milky way were breathtakingly beautiful. And a crescent moon. Perfect! The moon is visible most nights, and some days. Yet it has no light of its own. What we see is reflected light from the sun.

One of the loveliest spots in the United States, to me, is the lake at Maroon Bells in Colorado. Especially in early autumn, when the aspen trees are brassy gold. We have some photographs where it is almost impossible to tell which is the reflection in the lake, and which is the mountains and the trees.

People shine, too. Sometimes because of our own efforts. Yet humanism is not the best light we produce. The most lit up we are is when we are reflecting Jesus. No doubt about it, the shekinah glory, 'Son' light is reflection of the purest, finest, and brightest of God's light. What a great way to effortlessly shine, and maybe attract others to the Real Light - not just the reflection.

He..rebuked the wind and the raging waters; the storm subsided, and all was calm.   Luke 8:25

Rough Waters

Recently my husband was in Marathon, 'the heart of the beautiful Florida Keys', for a fishing trip with some guys. He said it was windy and really rough out. I could picture the boat getting slammed with the waves. Ordinarily, he wouldn't have even left the dock in this kind of weather, but the men were only there a brief time (so they 'had to do it').

According to Ben, an experienced fisherman, calm waters are usually close in to shore, near the land which protects it. The rougher waters are out farther, in between the shallow and the deep, over the reefs. The depth of the water, however, isn't what matters in how rough it is. Interestingly, more fish are usually caught in these rougher waters.

This particular day they were offshore about nine miles. The men got a banner catch that day, a bull dolphin and some schoolies. A marlin even took the bait, which is rare for this time of year.

I doubt anyone wants to get banged up and bruised from the 'rough waters' we all encounter in life. Nor be nervous, or afraid, to say nothing of perhaps not being able to 'fish'.

The rough waters we have can be calmed by the protective shore of Jesus, who is always there. He spoke to the elements in nature, and they obeyed. He can also speak to our hearts, and supernatural calm can replace our rough waters.

That is good news.

For the word of God is living and active. Sharper than any double-edged sword, it penetrates even to dividing soul and spirit, joints and marrow; it judges the thoughts and attitudes of the heart.   Hebrews 4:12

Rounds

In our back yard we have 2 bird feeders. Since I try to attract cardinals, I keep them filled with sunflower seeds. Early in the mornings, or late in the afternoons, the birds make their rounds. Seems as if they spend all their time looking for food. From one feeder to another, they are continually hunting for something to eat.

On the other hand, my dog will eat anything. Well, except dill pickles. And she doesn't much like olives either. But she will eat anything else. Lettuce. Tomatoes. She'll even lick a lemon. She's not picky about what she eats, or how much she eats.

We sometimes make the rounds looking for spiritual "food". We go from place to place, from New Age literature to Zen, trying to find something that will satisfy us.

But nothing seems to. Except the Bible. We don't have to settle for just anything in our searching for spiritual nourishment. The Word of God is right in front of us all the time.

There's a saying, "Don't read just any book, read the best". Spiritually speaking, we have a smorgasbord of the best food available to us in the Bible. We can literally feast to our hearts' content, and be glad we did!

Do I make use of the very best "food" there is? Not nearly enough. Thank God we have it! And I resolve (again) to go there first.....before I make the rounds.

For this reason he had to be made like his brothers in every way.... Hebrews 2:17

Seeking Understanding

When I was a lot younger and my Mom would be trying to drive home a point with me, she would say, "Someday when YOU are a mother, you will understand." These days my daughter will occasionally say to me, "Now that I'm a Mom, I understand you a lot better!"

You have to "be there" to "get it". No one can really understand outside of experientially. You can have all the head knowledge in the world, but until you experience some things, there's just no way you can understand them.

A long time ago, about 2000 years, God fulfilled a plan He'd had since way back in the Garden of Eden. He became a person, because He wanted to reconcile us to Himself.

That was the plan. So - Jesus, God in the flesh, was born as a little tiny baby. He grew up in a family and experienced every single thing that every person does.

We're all pretty much alike when you get right down to it. Solomon, the wisest man who ever lived and author of Ecclesiastes, said: *"There is nothing new under the sun."*

Jesus understands us, because He's "been there". So whenever we are seeking understanding, we can remember Someone is right here to do that very thing.

*She gave birth to her firstborn, a son. She wrapped him in
cloths and placed him in a manger. Luke 2:5-7*

Someone Else's Birthday

In January this past year, I received an email from a family
friend, a young mom who was commenting on her toddler's take
on Christmas: "I think Zander will really look forward to
Christmas next year - now that he gets it - on the kid level
anyway. He knows it is Jesus' Birthday and I think he's pretty
impressed that on someone else's birthday - he gets all the gifts!"

Short and sweet. Profound truth. The "kid level" is where I hope
I'm at when this time of year rolls around. For a lot of reasons,
particularly because it's Someone else's birthday.

"If you knew the gift of God... you would have asked him and he would have given you living water."   John 4:10

Something in the Water

Large clumps of hot pink pentas are planted in the round clay pots on our back deck. They are hardy flowers, as well as butterfly attractors. Yesterday afternoon I was in the yard and noticed all the brown leaves on them. "It looks as if they're dying", I thought. "What in the world?"

An instant replay ran in my mind. The kids making dirt pies and leaves and flower soup over in that area. And oh yes, helping Grandma water the plants! That means taking bucketsful of pool water and dumping them on the pentas.

For a time, the plants flourished. Apparently, however, there is something in the water that didn't agree with them, perhaps the chlorine in the pool water. And it got 'em.

Living water; we all need it. If you're drinking any other kind, it will eventually get ya. And the good news is that the 'something' in living water is available for free, to anyone, anytime.

The Lord is close to the brokenhearted and saves those who are crushed in spirit.   Psalm 34:18

Something You Never Had

Cindy waited 34 long years and stayed in the marriage. She gave it her all, and waited for her husband to come around. He was emotionally unavailable. He dropped dead from a heart attack last month. Bye-bye to that hope. Sam is 58 years old. There's been a hole in his heart as big as all outdoors for 56 of those years, wanting his father who disappeared when he was two. Dianne has been looking for someone to come into her life for many years. A partner and lover. She is old now. It may not happen.

Have you ever longed for something you've never had? Something money can't buy? Maybe a good relationship with your mother or father, or your kids. Perhaps you would really like a relationship that is now impossible, because that person has died.

You can be sad about something you never had. You can grieve something you never will have. But can you lose something you never had?

One thing you could never lose - even if you wanted to - the unconditional love that God your Father has for you. Never. No way! Not possible to lose that; it's there for ever and ever. It's just for you.

The LOVE that GOD has for YOU is not, and never could be, something you never had. It's been there all of your life. Even before. And it will be after.

Just ask him to show you. He will!

You will be a crown of splendor in the Lord's hand, a royal diadem in the hand of your God.   Isaiah 62:3

Sparkle and Shimmer

Those skinny white-trunked trees, related to the birches, are aspens. They are so beautiful. In summer, the heart shaped leaves are a lustrous green on top; the underside is a flat grayish green. As the breeze flutters through, the leaves sparkle and shimmer like no other tree. It is so eye-catching!

In autumn, the leaves turn a glorious gold, and when those small trees are massed together all over the face of a mountain, it is breathtaking.

Individually, we are - each one - beautiful, too. We are jewels, created by God, precious, priceless, and irreplaceable. When the breeze of God's Holy Spirit blows on us and through us, we sparkle and shimmer. It, too, is so eye-catching! Sparkling and shimmering - what a great way to effortlessly shine -and share - the love and beauty of God!

If you do not have a personal relationship with Him, seek Him today. Ask Him to send His spirit through you, like the breeze through the aspens. He will.

This is what the Lord says, he who created you, he who formed you: Fear not, for I have redeemed you; I have summoned you by name; you are mine. Isaiah 43:1

Stand Out Rose

On the side of our house, my husband has a rose garden. He plants, prunes, fertilizes, and sprays the small bushes. We so enjoy the beauty of the blooms, as well as their wonderful fragrance.

A few months ago, he set 2 or 3 of the rose bushes, still in plastic pots, aside. They were nearly dead and he planned to throw them away, but he forgot. So they stayed there, and they became overgrown with tall grass and weeds.

Today when I opened the mini-blinds, I immediately noticed this tiny rose bud outside the window. It stood out because of the bright color, in contrast to the dark shades of green all around it. The stem was about a foot high, and the little flower a beautiful pinkish-orange hue.

There it was, rising out of the midst of the stubble and weeds. It's amazing what God can grow out of an overgrown cast-off pot. HE is the One who can grow something beautiful out of anything, and in everyone. In fact, He is just waiting for the chance for us to let Him.

That's good news!

He who began a good work in you will carry it on to completion.....   Philippians 1:6

Stretched

"How did I get into this?" I wondered. I was going to a conference with someone I don't know well. Plans had changed a hundred times. Even now, at the last minute, they were changing. The phone calls and emails were flying back and forth. First one thing, then another. How about earlier? What about later? Maybe we should eat first? When can we actually check in?

The timing's terrible, I thought. I just took my last provera, and I'm on the brink of insanity; I am in no mood for this!

The telephone rang - her again? Providentially, it was a friend from out of state. She said my name had just come up on her caller ID, so she was returning my call. I hadn't called her in days. Aha! Maybe an angel had posted my name on her answer machine so she would call just then?

After we talked and she prayed for me, it hit me. This conference thing wasn't just another hair-raising situation. It was an opportunity for me to say "Yes" to God. He was doing what He does: attempting to grow me up a little bit more spiritually. He was stretching me.

The story has a happy ending. We made it to our destination on time, had a marvelous weekend, and became fast friends in the Lord.

God will use whatever He wants to accomplish His will for us, which is to stretch and grow us into the likeness of Himself. And He is relentless. Thank God!

In him was life, and that life was the light of men. John 1:4

Switched On

When I came inside, the house was pitch dark. I had forgotten to leave even the small table lamp on. Flicked the switch; no light. I wondered, "Is that bulb out again? It was just changed!".

To be certain, I put in a new bulb. Wasn't that. Maybe the plug wasn't in the socket tight? I checked that...no, it was intact and OK. "The fuse box! Must be that." Yup......I threw the switches, and voila! There was light.

The whole concept of 'light' is very interesting. It is amazing that one tiny spark of light will dissipate darkness. In the Bible, in the 1st chapter of John, we read that John the Baptist was not THE light but one who came to bear witness to the light . Then in Matthew 5 it says, "You are the light of the world....let your light shine before men, that they may ...praise your Father in heaven."

Yes, we are the light as well! And when our fuse boxes are functioning and our power supply active, our lights are clearly visible.

We can be as shiny and as pretty as everything, yet without Holy Spirit power we are being lit up under our own steam.

How much more genuine and bright are our lights when we are switched on by THE power source of Light, the Holy Spirit?!

So stay "switched on" and "let your little light shine; let it shine, let it shine, let it shine"!

Let us hold unswervingly to the hope we profess, for he who promised is faithful.   Hebrews 10:23

The Ant Scout

We have this continual thing with ants at our house. Here's how it seems to work: the ants have a secret place they live, hidden in the wall, or behind the cabinets, or light switch or "Somewhere". They frequently dispatch a "scout " to check out the counter tops and sink for any food bits. The scout meanders around, and should he find anything of interest, he returns to the nest to alert the others. At that point the steady stream begins, with the ants transporting the booty to their home.

My theory is if I catch the scout, no more ants will follow. Reminds me of the saying, "Don't kill the messenger". He's not the bad guy. He only showed up to deliver the message.

Long time ago God sent someone to us. He wasn't bad; in fact he was as good, loving, kind and perfect as anyone could be. Yet we killed him.

There's a happy ending though, to this story. God's messenger was Jesus, God's son. And his death and subsequent resurrection is what brings us life- forever.

Perhaps from now on when I see an ant scout, it will remind me of the good news of The Messenger.

You are precious and honored in my sight, and... I love you.
Isaiah 43:4

The Candy Shelves

She was maybe 5 or 6. She was waiting for her mom there in the drugstore, and she was standing near the cash register with her eyes glued to the candy shelves. For that little girl, paradise was just a few feet and a few dimes away.

Different times, different things. When we are little we want our bottle. Grade school we want to only be with our friends. Teenagers want romance, and ... a car! Then we want a job, a home, a family. And a fulfilling life. Happiness. Security in a changing world. Retirement investments. Good health.

Throughout all our ages and stages we want a LOT of different things. But God always wants the same thing. Us.

In the Bible, God tells us that He created us for fellowship with Him, and He relentlessly pursues us and that relationship. We are restless in our spirits until we are "with Him".

He won't give up, and He won't give in. He will continue to lovingly gaze upon you as if you, yourself, are those candy shelves.

He calls his own sheep by name and leads them out..He goes on ahead of them, and his sheep follow him because they know his voice.   John 10:3-4

The Voice

We were sitting around rehashing ball games, slumber parties, teachers, and who went steady with whom. Yup, we were getting ready for another class reunion. How do they come around so often? Every 10 or 20 years; doesn't seem like they ought to crop up so "often!"

The last reunion, I remember thinking that the guys had definitely changed more than the girls had, especially in the hair department! I recall looking at the Yearbook picture name tags; how memories came flooding back.

One thing stands out most in my mind from that reunion. Although most of our appearances were drastically different from high school days, one thing had not changed one iota. That was our voices. I discovered I could identify people when I heard them speak, even if I didn't recognize them from the way they looked.

How interesting. I thought of what Jesus said: the sheep listen to the shepherd's voice, and they follow him because they know his voice. They will never follow a stranger, because they don't recognize his voice.

How great to think that as we listen to the voice of our own shepherd, Jesus, and follow him, we won't get mis-led or go off in the wrong direction.

He is speaking, and we know His voice. It is Love, and it never changes.

That is good news.

".... how much more will your Father in heaven give the Holy Spirit to those who ask him!"   *Luke 11:13*

The Watering Hole

Here in sunny south Florida we have had the most beautiful winter we have had in years. It has been cool, clear, and purely delightful. However it has been majorly dry. This morning I saw one of the squirrels, who nests high up in one of the coconut palms, coming towards the wood deck.

On the decking, there's a defunct jacuzzi under an old canvas cover, which is so stretched it has pockets that hold water. The doves around dusk, and the squirrels, apparently regard this as their watering hole. As this little squirrel approached, he peered into what was a pitiful tiny bit of a pool. He bent over and drank what he could. Could be my imagination, but it seemed to me he acted disappointed as he went off in search of water some other place.

In our country we are usually able to access water through our faucets. Occasions such as hurricanes, water mains bursting and bacteria entering, have all brought to my attention how precious drinking water becomes when it can't be taken for granted.

We can live without food, but not without water. Jesus said we can have 'living water' (John 4). Spiritually speaking, we can't live without that kind of water, either. How fortunate we are to have free access to that 'water', the gift of the Holy Spirit through Jesus Christ.

I am so very grateful I can keep on drinking at this wonderful watering hole of living water, that our loving heavenly father has provided for all of us, anytime, anywhere.

Both the one who makes men holy and those who are made holy are of the same family. So Jesus is not ashamed to call them brothers.   Hebrews 2:11

Thicker Than Water

"Blood is thicker than water". That's an expression I've heard all my life. "When the chips are down, you can count on your family."

My parents taught us that our family may not like or approve of what we do, but they don't throw in the towel, walk away, and disown us. When the chips are down, even if friends desert you, family will stand by you. Others can help, but family, relatives, kinfolk ...it's best to turn to them if at all possible.

It is very cool that Jesus is twice a blood relative. First, we're both children of Abraham. Second, He sacrificed his life and shed his blood on Calvary, making it possible for us to be reconciled to our Father God. In fact God adopted us, making us brothers and sisters with Jesus. Family.

The church universal, the body of Christ, is our family, too! There's an old Gaither song that goes something like, "....I've been washed in His goodness, washed in his blood; joint heirs with Jesus as we travel along, we're part of the family, the family of God."

Last summer I received this email from a friend in Michigan: "The family reunion is well under way this whollllllle week.

All 30 of us park on our dock and eat from our kitchen.   While it has been nice I am ready to say so-long. Our golf cart was driven into a creek by a nephew (that was on my side), one of my nieces broke the boat key in half (my husband's side). Two nephews collided in jet skies and damaged one completely....thank God not themselves too badly. Oh family life!"

Regardless, family is beautiful. The Bible encourages, in chapter 6 of the book of Galatians......*as we have opportunity, let us do good to all people, especially to those who belong to the family of believers.*

Blood brothers and sisters in the Lord. Thank God, blood IS thicker than water, and exceedingly priceless.

The fear of the Lord is the beginning of knowledge, but fools despise wisdom and discipline.   Proverbs 1:7

Time Out

Remember when 'time out' was when the umpire called for a break? Then maybe you're as old as I am. The little blue chair, off to the side in my daughter's family room, is the "time out" spot. She has used it on only a few occasions. Her 2 1/2 year old quickly connected sitting there with disciplinary action.

Last winter my husband I and I rented a condo on our vacation. I saw the pictures in the bedroom, but it wasn't until we had been there several days that I really looked at them, while resting, and simply being still. Interesting, I thought, how you have to get quiet to really see.

Same with snorkeling. We don't do much of it anymore, but our family used to. It is so quiet under the surface of the water. And if you stay still, and hover over a reef, it is amazing and wonderful what comes out and what you notice.

Likewise with the Word. The bible says, "Be still." I add, "and look at what you see with your spiritual eyes, the eyes of your soul".

For sure I need to discipline myself. Sitting still, looking, seeing, doesn't come too naturally for me. I enjoy being on the move. However, setting aside just ten minutes, and putting my own self in 'time out', is bound to make a difference.

I will ask the Father, and he will give you another Counselor to be with you forever - the Spirit of truth.   John 14:16-17

Traveling Companion

The small potty chair traveled everywhere my young grandson went. His mom was potty-training him. So the day they came over for a swim, they arrived with the mini-potty in tow. Ryan had on swim diapers, however the little potty was handy at the side of the pool. My daughter would haul it around; it was never very far away from wherever her toddler was.

We are in training, too. Faith training; the journey of our faith walk. No last chapter on that, not in this lifetime.

Fortunately we have someone who is with us everywhere we go: a guide, teacher, helper. The Holy Spirit is our constant traveling companion.

That is good news. Thank you, Jesus.

Let us then approach the throne of grace with confidence...
Hebrews 4:16

Waltz In

I was praying. Simple conversation with God. And found myself asking Him for something again. I thought, "I am constantly making requests. Wouldn't you think He would get sick of that? I just waltz in, any time of the day or night I feel like it, and ask Him for something . And just assume He will listen, and do it. "

Years ago, as a mom of young children, I would try to stop and listen to my kids when they would come to me to ask, or tell, me something. I usually did, but not always. Seemed that more often than not they wanted to talk when I was rushing to get dinner on the table, or bedtime, or another time that was less than convenient.

Our Father God made us for fellowship with Him. And yes, He is thrilled and delighted for us to come to Him, with requests, conversation, thanks, or just come to enjoy His presence. There's never a time the Lord won't stop and give us His full attention. In fact, He is just waiting for us to come.

So, waltz on in.

Trust in the Lord with all your heart, and lean not on your understanding; in all your ways acknowledge Him and will make your paths straight.   Proverbs 3:5-6

White Butterfly

My husband and I were threading our way down the path from our trek up to the waterfall. Nothing around. No people, no birds, no animals... except for one very small chipmunk scurrying from rock to rock to avoid our big scary shoes coming toward him.

Then a tiny white butterfly appeared. It fluttered along in front of us all, as if leading the way. All the way down the trail to the bridge at the bottom. There, by the river's edge, it flew into the woods, only to reappear behind us when we moved on.

We weren't lost. But sometimes we don't have to be completely lost to need a little guidance and direction. Or even reassurance.

Ten thousand feet up in the Rocky Mountains, could a white butterfly be a reminder saying God will go ahead of us to lead the way? And that He will also come behind us?

God tells us in the Bible, "I will never leave you or forsake you." (Joshua 1, Deuteronomy 31, Hebrews 13)

It's a promise! That's good news.

"I will be a Father to you, and you will be my sons and daughters, says the Lord Almighty." 2 Corinthians 6:18

Who Feels the Pain?

This week held a big step for two people close to me. My daughter had said, "I don't know if I can let him go!" And on Tuesday, my 3 yr. old grandson went to school for the first time. It's hard to say who felt the pain of separation more; my daughter, her first-born, or Grandma.

It was deja vu for me as I was transported back in time. Our oldest child began morning pre-school at the same age. I suspect the parent feels the pain more than the child. The youngster is on to new and exciting adventures, while the parent is left behind in his or her same routine.

Maybe it's always easier for the one who moves on than the one who is left. My friend Ed, a counselor, says you grieve when you lose a person, place, or thing. It could be just about anything in life, little or big.

I thought about who was it that felt the pain more when we became separated from God back in the Garden of Eden? And who grieved the most? My guess is that it was our father, God. His pain was unbearable enough to immediately set about implementing the plan He'd had since before the foundation of time to bring us back into that close former relationship with him.

It did finally happen. As all things came together, so long ago, Jesus became the bridge between us and our heavenly parent. Happy endings are always good, and there is none better than this one.

That is definitely good news.

Jesus Christ is the same yesterday and today and forever.
Hebrews 13:8

Winds of Change

The winds of change are blowing in our home. We have enjoyed a season of peace and calm without sickness or tragedy. Now, however change is in the wind. Circumstances are stirring with my husband's job. So far it is a breeze, not a full gale hurricane.

Everything is for a season, the good times as well as the bad times. Each change brings something new. That is always a bit difficult for me. Certain, yes. Predictable, yes. Yet the unknown is still a little scary.

In the Bible, we read that God is the same yesterday, today, and forever. In the book of Matthew (28:20), Jesus promises that the same faithful God who is with us today will be with us in the newness of tomorrow. We don't have to be alone! That takes the fear out of it.

I have to remind myself, sometimes daily, that when I feel anxious, I have jumped into the future. Staying rooted in the moment will make anxiety flee. I need to ask the Lord to send an angel to hold my feet and ankles and help keep me grounded in the present.

We cannot go anywhere God is not already there. So blow, winds of change.

Repent, then, and turn to God, so that your sins may be wiped out, that times of refreshing may come from the Lord.   Acts 3:19

Fresh

Showered and pressed, I felt fresh as a crisp autumn morning. I arrived at the airport early. With few people in line at that hour, getting through check-in and the scanners was smooth and quick.

At the newstand, I went in to get a new paperback mystery and a candy bar, then headed down the concourse. Soon the smell of grease was strong. It hung heavy in the stale airport air. Looking around, I saw a fast-food shop, still closed. The poorly ventilated restaurant was the culprit.

My gate was across the aisle. As I sat there I could sense that odor permeating my clothes and hair. I had started out clean, but it wasn't going to last long. I'd need another shower by the time I arrived at the conference hotel. I thought of how, spiritually, I can be determined, purposed, cleaned up and refreshed, and how it doesn't last that long. Just about daily I have to renew my determination, etc.

The Bible has great wisdom and wonderful practical advice on many things, including this subject. Yes, I want to choose spiritual refreshing, so I'll be fresh as a crisp autumn morning, from the inside out.

Do not be anxious about anything, but in everything, by prayer and petition, with thanksgiving, present your requests to God. Philippians 4:6

Getting It Just Right

My husband enjoys relaxing in the living room, listening to me play the piano. Amateur though it is, I try to get it just right. He is gracious, and praises my playing, then I try even harder.

One year for his birthday, I planned to surprise him with a tape of me playing his favorite songs. Oh boy! Was that ever a project! Taping, re-taping, and patching it into my hand-held recorder was more than tedious. Still, I wanted to get it just right.

My piano playing is riddled with mistakes, yet to my husband it sounds wonderful. He doesn't notice the errors. He simply enjoys the music I am making.

How often we want to do everything just right for our heavenly father. We want to please him, be as good and nice as possible, make him proud of us. Because we are human, we can never be perfect and do everything just right. However, what is so cool is that in God's eyes, we are perfect. He loves us just as we are, and sees us as we will be.

What a relief we don't have to get everything just right for Him. God has already gotten everything just right for us. When we believe in Jesus, and His sacrifice for us, it all falls into place. Perfectly.

That is good news.

If you....know how to give good gifts to your children, how much more will your Father in heaven give good gifts to those who ask him!   Matthew 7:11

Gifts

Maybe we give gifts according to where we are at the time, rather than where the person is who is getting the gift.

Last week, I bought the loveliest handkerchief for my sister. It is old-fashioned looking and has her initial on it.. I was in a nostalgic and sentimental mood at the time. She's not a very frilly of fluffy person. But she will probably like it.

This afternoon, I bought my friend some smiley face pencils for her birthday. I like them, and although smiley face is not her favorite she will no doubt appreciate the thought behind it.

A long time ago, our Father decided to give us a gift. He picked something He wanted to give us: a bridge back to Him, and the relationship He has always wanted with us. It cost Him a bundle, but He gave us the gift anyway, because that's where He was at......loving us that much.

Give thanks to the Lord for He is good; His love endures forever.   Psalm 107:1

Good to Know

At Thanksgiving.......... Turkey. Pilgrims. Indians. Cranberry jelly. Don't forget the pumpkin pie.

Thanksgiving. A good time to ask myself, what am I thankful for? Even better, whom should I thank?

Parents, spouse, children family, home, things, jobs, clothes, food, stuff, friends, health, life itself. Everything we want - and need - in our lives.

Often it looks like it's a person who deserves our thanks. Sometimes we think circumstance gets the credit. Yet ultimately, everything we have is a gift from God. Even who we are is a gift from God.

God uses people and situations to channel his gifts to us. He alone is the Great Gift-giver.

It is good to know Whom to thank.

Then God said, "Let us make man in our image, in our likeness..
So God created man in his own image   Genesis 1:26-27

Handmade

Maybe it sounds corny, but I like handmade presents best. Not
to say I don't like silver and sparkly, but a handmade gift is a
treasured bit of the gift-giver.

This past Christmas I received a card from Taylor, my eleven
year old granddaughter. It was special because she thought of it,
she created it with love, customized it just for me, and gave it to
me. Another special present was a double picture frame, with 2
photos in it, from my sister. The old black and white on the left
is the two of us when we were really young. On the right is a
photo of us at my birthday recently. A special gift, handmade
with love, and holding countless memories.

Do you know we are handmade gifts? To the world, and to each
other. God made us, and we know that without Him nothing was
made that was made.

Handmade gifts. Sharing the heart and soul of the giver.
Handmade.....the best.

Though she (a mother) may forget, I will not forget you! See, I have engraved you on the palms of my hands. Isaiah 49:15-16

He Didn't Know Me

Stopping by for a quick visit, I was surprised to find the house unlocked and no one home. Out back, in an open patch by the road, I found my 89 year old dad. He was sitting on a towel, trimming the grass, with a pair of small scissors. I said, "Hi!" He looked up at me with vacant eyes. For a minute, he didn't know me.

My heart lurched. If you've been there, you know what I'm talking about. If you haven't, perhaps one day you will be blessed with this situation.

I didn't used to look at things this way. Then I heard a wise woman say, "Everything is a gift from God." it was the 'everything' that got my attention.

In heaven, my dad will know me again. And while I'm still here on earth, I can count on the truth that my heavenly Father will always recognize and love me, no matter how often I visit Him.

Acknowledgements

Of all the gifts the Lord has blessed me with, my family is the best:

To my husband, Ben, with all my love

To my children, with love beyond words -
Adie, David, Lisa, Todd, Teri, Benjie

And my precious grandchildren, with untold love -
Abby, Tommy, and Ryan Haag, Jackson, McCallen, and
Taylor Kennedy, Michael, Benjamin, and Courtney
Kennedy

To my favorite sister, Marion Smith, who keeps me on
track and laughing ... hope I can come to your birthday
party ☺

To long time friend, Shirley Rollins - TCB

To my magical, musical friend, Anne Woehle

To prayer warrior and friend, Mary Jo Clouse

To special mentor and friend, Edie Roach

To my funniest friend, Kitty LaRue Eggplant, aka Sandy
LeSourd

To dear friend, Lillian Saunders, much love from the Rev

To Gigi Graham, for many years of precious friendship

To the best neighbors ever, Carol and George Karas

To friend and champion of women for Jesus', Lee Grady

To Lynn Cleveland, for all the beautiful prayers and armor

To Jim Decker, for the wonderful website

To Jonathan Benz, for encouragement, ministry, and friendship

To Dody Ashman, for always supporting me and all my projects

To Fr. Joe Girzone, for first awakening in me the realness of Jesus

To Mickey and Ron Dingle, our dear anniversary friends

To Carolyn Morgan, my very dear friend

To dear friends/pastor, Susan and Andy Hagen

To my author girlfriend who named Irish Thursdays, Barbara Lundy

To my Lord, Savior, Friend, Redeemer-Jesus,
and with gratitude to my most wonderful Abba, and my
Friend, Holy Spirit- giving back what You have first given
me.

About The Author

"Your eyes are the windows of your inner-man. The intriguing artistry of Sally's devotionals will warm your soul to receive insights about life and spirituality that will nourish and soothe your spirit. " -**Jim Croft, Author/Pastor, The Heritage Factor www.jimcroftministries.com**

"Learn daily how to deal with life's exciting challenges. This book is filled with funny, insightful and practical Bible verses that will give you keys to turning the negative into the positive. Based on lessons learned and good time experiences from the heart of a Mother, Grandmother and woman with a heart after God. " -**Mary Jo Clouse, Author/Speaker, Clouse Restoration Ministries www.totalhealing.org**

"Sally Kennedy is one of those versatile and talented people; the birth of her newest creative effort, "Irish Thursdays" is charming and perceptive. Sally's devotionals are now sent via

internet to thousands of persons in over 25 countries. The fun thing about Sally's writing is it's like sitting down by a cozy fireplace having a cup of tea with her. It's an intimate look at a very wise woman, who knows God's Word and lives it. This weekly ministry has changed lives. I believe it will change yours as you meditate on these pages." -**Sandra LeSourd, author, The Compulsive Woman**

"Sally Kennedy's "Irish Thursdays" is not only strongly inspirational, but also beautifully written. Her descriptions give the reader a strong sense of place, almost as if we were there with her. She writes her devotionals, not for theologians and doctors of divinity, but rather so that every person who reads them can benefit spiritually, get insight into his own life and grow closer to his God." -**Robin G. Mahfood, President/CEO of Food For The Poor, Inc.**

"Stroll down the path of life- hand in hand with our heavenly Father- as Sally reflects the heart of God. Her teachings are interwoven with everyday experiences, and the peaceful photography, her own. This is a book that will enrich your spiritual life! " -**Marion Smith, author, Glimpses From God, and children's series, "Frank"**

"Sally Kennedy's devotional pieces have blessed me and countless others. Be "blessed" by them in her new book, "Irish Thursdays." They are spiritual masterpieces that dwell on God's Goodness & Love, written in a simple and "down to earth" manner." -**Nick Ledesma, Philippines**

"Like a fresh breath of the Holy Spirit, Irish Thursdays has greeted many of us with a delightful breeze of biblical insights, personal reflections, and abiding faith. Very few people have the gift to share the Spirit so simply and joyfully as Sally Kennedy. Read on and catch the wind that will lead you from Thursdays to everyday in the blessing of the Spirit." -**Andy Hagen, pastor, Advent Lutheran Church www.adventelca.org**

"Sally has the unique God-given talent of writing in a manner that grips and holds your attention. Her stories are blessings that remain in memory long after they are read." **-Bob, founder and publisher of Christian Voices**
www.ChristianVoicesWorldwide.com

"One of the resources I use weekly is "Irish Thursday" published by Sally I. Kennedy. Sally authors many outstanding Internet and hard copy publications; her work is outstanding and worthy of the read." **-George A. Ross, The Daily Message**

♥

Sally Ireland Kennedy is the author of *52 Little Parables from Ireland, Words from the Heart,* and *Kwackie the Wonder Duck.*

She a regular contributing writer to *Daily Wisdom,* as well as several E-zines and devotional sites, including *Friends Reflections, Food for Thought, Sermon Illustrator,* and *Just A Minute.*

Sally is an ordained minister, conference speaker, and the creator/songwriter for *Poppy the Penguin®,* a preschool music video series.

Sally and her husband, Ben, live in south Florida. They have three children and nine grandchildren.

Irish Thursdays: *More Little Parables from Ireland*

www.ingramcontent.com/pod-product-compliance
Lightning Source LLC
Chambersburg PA
CBHW031848090426
42741CB00005B/399